Not That High and
Not That Difficult

Araceli Segarra

Not That High and Not That Difficult

Foreword by Jamling Tensing Norgay

First edition September 2019
ISBN KDP AMAZON
ISBN: 9781688901971

A few words from Jamling

It has been nearly 22 years since the worst disaster happened on mt. Everest.

Many books have been written on the accounts of the events that transpired since then.

i felt proud to be a part of the IMAX filming team where we would take the large format IMAX cameras to the top of the world for the first time.

The journey to the top of the world was one to remember, and how we got there was more important. it was a team effort with a team of climbers being selected form around the world. one of them i got to climb with and got to know well was araceli, she was a woman of dynamic character very passionate about what she did and most importantly loved every minute of it.

It was my pleasure to have been climbing with araceli and for the both of us to have reached the summit of Everest together. she is a woman with great energy and continued to do so even after Everest.

araceli, is an explorer, a pioneer and a great team player. her adventures have taken her to the corners of the world including the high Himalayas including Everest, k2, and Kanchenjunga, the three highest mountains in the world.

I know this book reflects back on her past experiences and untold stories of her vast experiences.

this book will take you along a journey that few have taken and many have not known about.

Jamling Tenzing Norgay

Norgay is the son of **Nepali** mountaineer and guide **Tenzing Norgay** (who first climbed **Mount Everest** in 1953 with **Sir Edmund Hillary**)

Only those who will risk going too far
can possibly find out how far one can go.
T.S. ELIOT

I. An Ending to Start With.

I learned that courage was not the absence of fear, but the triumph over it. The brave man is not he who does not feel afraid, but he who conquers that fear.

NELSON MANDELA

I have never liked figs. Either as fruit or, what's worse, in the form of biscuits. Even so, today, for breakfast, I ate nearly a whole boxful. I ate the biscuits one by one while boiling the water to make tea. It was the only thing I felt like eating.

I say breakfast, but in fact I'd got up at eleven o'clock at night and right now, as I sit at the tent door, it's midnight. The darkness is absolute and outside it's bitterly cold. I hear noises from the other tents, but the wind prevents me from hearing them properly.

They are far away and I can't see who they are.

I feel dizzy. Yesterday, I hardly ate a thing.

I put my boots on and got into my down suit inside the tent. Now that I'm outside, I'm not sure if I'll be able to put on my crampons while wearing gloves. I'm wearing two pairs, thin gloves inside some thick mittens that make my hands hopelessly clumsy.

After having spent so much time studying and testing the materials, I suspect I've made a right mess of it all.

I decide to put my crampons on wearing just the thin gloves. There's a risk that my hands might get frozen, but I don't think there's really much chance of that. I'm properly hydrated, I've slept for four hours and I'm about to move out. After weighing up the options, I reckon that if I try and put the crampons on with the mittens, not only is it going to take a long time, but there's a chance I won't be able to fasten them securely.

At this altitude, each decision, every movement needs to be carefully calculated and evaluated. I'm well aware that up here, everything needs to be planned down to the last millimeter.

I'm at a height of almost 8,000 meters. It's midnight. It's pitch black, windy and extremely cold. I feel nauseous and I've got a loose stomach. I have difficulty breathing. I'm on my own and I have to make it to the summit of Everest.

For a moment, I think: "What the hell am I doing here?"

Right now I have the sensation that this isn't going to be at all easy. I know that it isn't impossible either, but it's going to be extremely uncomfortable and very tough.

It's all too much for me and I'm dog tired. I have to make an effort to overcome the inertia that is trying to keep me back in here, in the sleeping bag, inside the tent. That would be the easy way out, but I'm not going to do it because at this stage in the proceedings, after an expedition lasting two months, I've learnt a lot. Among other things, I now know the best option isn't always the easiest one.

THE DECISIVE PUSH

What is it, exactly, that enables us to make that final, decisive move? That split second which makes all the difference, when we hesitate to do something or not do it? It's like that moment when we decide to dive into the icy water of a lake or a swimming-pool. The decisive push.

I've thought about this often and have come to the conclusion that there are three factors which contribute to this final impulse:

1) **Experience** tells you that you've done it before, that the initial pain will disappear, that once you've dived into the pool you won't notice the cold anymore. Because you've been in the same situation many times before and you know that you can do it.

2) **The excitement about the reward** is about being aware that you're there, in the adventure that life is, for a reason. You're looking for something, and the wish to get what you want is stronger than your lethargy or the toughness or the suffering involved in the situation.

3) **Knowing that, if you don't try, you'll feel disappointed with yourself.** The shame and the disillusionment generated by not doing something is crueler and more painful than failing when you do try it.

These are the three ingredients that make up the decisive push, but in order for the result to be a success we need the magic of **conviction**. Aside from the necessary **preparation, effort and the ability to withstand adversity,** in order to meet any kind of challenge you first have to believe that you can do it.

If Edison paid attention to all the people who told him it was ridiculous to try and make a bulb that lit up, maybe we'd still be getting light from torches and oil lamps. **He did what he did because he didn't think it was impossible:** that was his secret.

Henry Ford said that que **"Whether you think you can, or you think you can't – you're right"** That moment when we tell ourselves "I can", before we dive into the swimming pool, is the result of conviction.

Let's take an extreme case, such as that of Felix Baumgartner, who broke the sound barrier with his body alone, in freefall, after jumping from outside the atmosphere at an altitude of over 36,000 meters. In the interviews he gave afterwards, he admitted that when he opened the hatch of his capsule he almost gave up. The visor of his helmet froze up at once, so that he couldn't see a thing. He lost his self-assurance and felt frightened. After all, he was about to do something that nobody else had ever tried.

He found himself facing that decisive moment in everybody's life: the final push. And this isn't something which only happens to inventors, mountaineers or people who throw themselves into the sky without knowing if their parachute's going to open. None of us would have been born if our father or mother hadn't made the decision to approach that other person who they liked so much. The decisive push changed everything and thanks to that moment of courage, we are here.

Which is why, when we're paralyzed by fear, it's worth remembering the motto of the Scottish essayist Thomas Carlyle: **Do not say that it is impossible. Say that you have not tried it yet. "**

Skating on Everest

I start walking, although it feels like an unwanted skating session. The ice is extremely hard on the stretch that goes from the tents to the beginning of the slope, and I'm wearing crampons that have been blunted by use. When I start sliding about, I can hardly see where I'm putting my feet. My headlamp barely lights up the two meters in front of me.

I'm on my own. The others left quite a while ago and I've been left behind. My goggles are getting frosted over by the cold and I have no idea as to the whereabouts of the path which leads to the summit. What with the effort it took me to leave the tent and everything that's happening now, for the second time tonight I feel like giving everything up.

WHAT AM I DOING HERE?

We often feel tempted to give it all up. No matter how great our earlier expectations may have been, when something doesn't turn out the way we want it to, or we find ourselves having to deal with more problems than we'd expected, then we've already got an excuse to throw in the towel.

Calling it a day is always the easiest option.

When we find ourselves in a tricky situation, however, before we abandon all hope it's worth pausing for a moment so as to calm our thoughts, take a deep breath, put our thoughts in order and analyze what it is that we have to find a solution to. This is **the cure for a mental blockage: finding solutions to our problems, one by one,** without trying to do everything at once.

It often happens in life that after taking a risk, we end up asking ourselves: **"What am I doing here?"** This was the very question that the great traveler Bruce Chatwin would ask himself; at the end of his life, he reached the conclusion that it is precisely when you ask yourself that, that you start to learn something. It's a sign that we've abandoned our comfort zone. We've left the certainties and safety of the known world in order to **discover something new, both about the world and ourselves.**

First, I decide to take off my goggles. I wear them so as to stop the cold from damaging my eyes, but the glass has misted up and I can't see. Then I look for a strip of hard snow so that I can stop slipping and sliding. I immediately switch of my headlamp and try to locate the lights which are climbing ahead of me.

When I spot those of Jamling, David, Robert and the others, I start climbing in the same direction.

I'm frightened. I'm climbing on my own and it's dark; I try to follow their tracks through the rocks and snow. The worst thing of all is that I know that out here there are several very well-preserved corpses.

For some people, that isn't a problem. And everyone knows that the dead aren't going to do anything to you. All right, but imagine walking at night up a mountainside, knowing that close by there are three or four corpses, and you'll soon see that it isn't much fun.

The phantoms of fear

Yes, I'm afraid, but not of the mountain nor of what I'm doing. I know that, technically speaking, I'm competent enough to climb this mountain and come back down. The fear I feel is a ridiculous and absurd one. The dark doesn't scare me, I got over that a long time ago, when I started exploring caves at age fifteen. What I'm afraid of right now is coming across a dead body.

Repeatedly, and I'm not sure if it's by way of an obsession or a mantra, I check my entire body, so as to avoid making any mistakes. First, the feet; I check if they're cold or if my socks are wrinkled. Afterwards I move onto my hands; I move my fingers, checking them one by one, the thumb and the little finger, which are usually the first to freeze when you're holding an ice axe. Then I try to remember when I last drank some water.

I stop to check that my crampons are securely fastened, that there aren't any loose straps I could trip over.

At the same time, I think about plenty of other things. The corpses are one of the things that worry me most; I don't know exactly where they are, but I know they must be close.

As I move ahead, I decide I have to change my mental programming. I'm getting anxious and that involves an unnecessary loss of energy, so I search for something which will distract my thoughts until daybreak, to stop me thinking about the corpses of Rob Hall, Scott Fisher, the Japanese woman and the other dead people from the recent tragedy on Everest.

THINKING IS MORE TIRING THAN DOING

We're often not aware of how tiring it is to think about what we are about to do. When we've got a lot of work ahead of us, we get anxious because we think we won't be able to do it, or we get frightened by a challenge that we think we can't possibly face up to.

There's only way to get rid of this type of anxiety: **deal with things instead of fretting about them.**

In my case, when I'm beset by the phantoms of fear, or by exhaustion or pain, I always start to think about what needs to be done at that very moment. If you're concentrating on each step you take, the route, the way you push the crampons against the ground, the column of your colleagues who are making a dream come true, then your mental fatigue vanishes. All your energy is focused on the specific goal that you wish to achieve.

This a lesson that has proved very helpful to me in daily life. When I'm swamped with work, instead of thinking about it, I do it. **One thing after another.** As Lao Tse said, in his best-known adage: **"A thousand-mile journey begins with a single step."**

Lights in the darkness

I go on climbing, slowly. I've set a pace for myself and I stick to it. I only stop once an hour to drink, and while doing that, I take a look around.

I hear nothing but a fading gust of wind.

I see nothing but some little lights, some tiny dots. It's them. I am me. This silence. This isolation.

Knowing that I'm all alone in one of the most inhospitable places on the planet, without any kind of assistance to hand, makes me feel more alive than ever, luckier than ever just to exist. It's a miracle that millions of possibilities have come together to create a conscious being.

Caught up in this whirl of happiness and awareness, I begin to put everything into perspective. I see those little dots that are moving slowly ahead of me. And if one of them were to go out, what would that mean? What would it mean if my own light, my life, were to be extinguished right this instant?

Well, nothing. The world would keep on turning. The universe would continue to expand. It would mean absolutely nothing. We are not indispensable. We're not as important as we think. We are not the center of the universe. We are nothing more than tiny lights in the darkness.

Life is a gift and our obligation is to squeeze what we can out of it and to savour it down to the last drop. We need to live knowing that we are alive, breathe knowing that we exist. To waste our lives is an offence to the universe, no matter how old we are. An Irish proverb says: "Don't complain about getting old; many have been denied that privilege."

So there's no point in complaining, or in lazing about, or in spending time on things that don't matter, wasting a few moments when we don't know how long things are going to last.

I think about all this as I climb the slope to a height of 8,300 meters. At three in the morning, at twenty degrees below zero in the darkness, I experience a moment of lucidity that I've never felt before. Suddenly, I come to my senses and realize how lucky we are just to be alive.

THE LAST LESSON OUGHT TO BE THE FIRST

Many people have seen the light and understood the deeper truths of life after suffering an accident or a serious illness. Often, however, they're not in time to do what they'd have liked to. The lesson has arrived too late.

Why do we have put our lives in jeopardy, consciously or unconsciously, to realize all this? Be it because of a sport that we're doing, o because of an illness or an accident... It isn't until we stand on tiptoe at the edge of a precipice and understand that we might die, that we realize how much we love life.

It is in such moments of epiphany, of illumination, that we suddenly discover that what we wanted is precisely that which we are about to lose.

But can't there be a way of realizing this without taking risks or losing everything?

In his book *Tuesdays With Morrie*, the journalist *D*Mitch Albom explains his last conversations with a terminally ill man who teaches him the meaning of our allotted span of life: **doing and loving.** As the old master says: **"If you accept the fact that you could die at any moment, you will stop being so ambitious and open the door to love."**

The Mount Everest Balcony

A couple of hours after leaving the tent, I catch up with Jamling and, a little later, with Robert. I'm now in the column. We all keep a fair distance from each other and as there aren't many of us on the mountain – just ten – once again I have the feeling that I'm alone again. And I like that.

I don't know how I've managed to overtake the others. Perhaps because I can't see much, it was probably when someone stopped to drink and I overtook them in a flash.

I try to make a game out of everything in order to keep my concentration focused. I have to keep my mind awake and, above all, immune to unpleasant thoughts. I reach the Balcony, at 8,400 meters. How pretty the Lhotse Wall looks from here!

I sit down on the snow to wait for my fellow climbers. Maybe this isn't a good idea, but I don't make any effort to change my position; besides, I've never heard of anyone getting a frozen bum.

David, the director of the documentary, tells me this is one of the places where we're going to film, and that I have be patient until all the others have got here.

I look down and see Jamling coming up. Behind him, in the background, the South Col brightens in the reddish light of dawn. It's still freezing. From the Balcony I can see the tents of our last camp, Camp IV. They are nothing but dots.

I imagine the journey that Beck Weathers made when he woke up from a lethargic coma and managed to get to the tents, completely blind. What luck! If he'd varied his route by just a few degrees, he would have fallen off the precipice without fail; it was a miracle he kept to the right course without being able to see a thing.

Is there such a thing as luck?

The old camera and the large device

I turn around, and, behind me, I see an image of whose existence I'd been unaware: the shadow of the peak of Everest projected onto the horizon, over the clouds that are rising up in the Khumbu Valley, that valley of silence.

I take off my old, heavy camera. I bought it second-hand from the family of Òscar Ribes, a young man from Lleida who died many years ago on the Alpamayo, a pyramid of ice in the Peruvian Andes.

I like taking it to the mountains for two reasons: the first is that I'm sure its previous owner would have liked to know that his camera was still taking pictures of mountains; the second is that the probability that the same camera could have two owners both of whom die in the mountains strikes me as being so small, it makes me feel protected.

And I'm not at all superstitious, because that brings bad luck.

The camera is a mechanical Nikon, a relic that works with rolls of slides. Each time I take a photo, I have to make sure that I've measured the light correctly and that I've synchronized the aperture diaphragm with the shutter speed. I have no way of knowing if the image has come out well or not. And in this particular case, it'll take me two months to find out, until when I'm back in the United States and can develop the rolls of the entire expedition.

Now we're all together up here. Except that Ed's missing, the guy who left the camp a little earlier so as to mark out the path. And as he doesn't use oxygen, we all thought we'd catch him up in a few hours, but no way. He's like Speedy González.

Setting up the IMAX camera is a whole ritual. The rucksacks are placed on the snow, then they're opened carefully and the different pieces of the camera are fixed together.

I watch these manoeuvres with curiosity: with practice, they're carried out faster each time. Sometimes it's David and Robert who do them, often with the help of the porters or us.

We've tried to keep the weight of the equipment so we can move more quickly. That's why we've replaced the heavy tripod with a monopod. We're also carrying the minimum amount of film and batteries. Each roll of film lasts one minute only, and weighs about three kilos. And each battery weighs three kilos. That means we can't waste any material, we have to be exacting with the images and the takes. I learnt that in the course of an argument, the only one I remember having during the entire expedition.

The highest repeated take in the history of the cinema.

After having set up the camera, for the Balcony scene at 8,400 meters, and having put the film carefully in the camera before choosing the composition, the aperture of the diaphragm and the shutter speed, David sends me down the ridge so as to film me climbing back up. Jamling always walks behind me.

To my right is the dizzying East Face. I look at it and think: "Whoa, no way!" I won't go down this all but inaccessible slope. I hear the deafening sound of the camera's motor. It makes such a racket because it has to feed the big, heavy IMAX film through.

The sound of the noise is the signal to start walking. I've always wanted to hear "Attention, camera, action!" and be surrounded by a bunch of assistants and make-up girls, but I have to make do with the whir of this tractor-like sound and the sun block I put on this morning before setting off.

It takes me ages to reach the spot where the camera is, which is where I'm supposed to come to a halt. Once there, without realizing it I go faster than I should, walking straighter than I normally would. I suspect even my eyes are wider than normal.

Half lying down to rest, I put my hands on my knees. Then to my surprise, given that I thought we'd pack up the gear and keep on climbing, David starts yelling into my ear. It's impossible to understand his English, because he's furious, aphonic, and most important of all, he's wearing his oxygen mask.

I'm sick of listening to English, exhausted, and my balaclava is under the hood of my down suit. In other words, I don't exactly have an open channel of communication. I can't understand what he's saying! It takes me a while to comprehend that I haven't done the take the way I should have.

What haven't I done properly? The walking? What's the problem?

We haven't understood each other, for some reason. I didn't grasp which direction it was that he wanted me to take, and he probably didn't explain himself with the clarity that the moment required.

I've had to do the scene again. That's an impossible thing on any expedition: to go back twice in order to climb back up. To raise a heavy boot, with the crampons attached, is not a graceful move, and the less repeated, the better.

The second time around, having followed David's orders more carefully, he gives me the thumbs up. We have just shot the highest repeat take in the history of the cinema.

THE VITAMIN "C" OF TEAMWORK

Why do things sometimes turn out badly when we work as part of a team? That's something that happens everywhere: in the office, in a theatre company, in a football team or on a cinematographic expedition like ours. We often have the knowledge and skills required for the task we are carrying out, but even then, the result is not satisfactory.

In such cases, the problem is a failure in the channel of communication. The **"vitamin C"** which feeds the connections and cohesions within a group. Many of the conflicts and malfunctions of teamwork are the result of misunderstandings, due to insufficient communication. Very rarely is there an express wish to do things badly. Information is not correctly transmitted, either because it doesn't emerge clearly from its source, because it gets lost in route or because the receiver of the information doesn't interpret it correctly.

In his classic *L'illa dels 5 fars*, the communications expert Ferran Ramon Cortés, after a visit to Minorca's lighthouses, developed these **five keys to good communication.**

1) **A big single message** is far more effective and convincing than getting bogged down in lots of different issues, which will confuse the receiver.

2) **The content of the message must be expressed in a way which is memorable.** A personalized message, with stories or metaphors, will remain fixed in the minds of our listeners.

3) **We have to choose language that resonates with the listener.** The social and cultural characteristics of our interlocutor should be borne in mind, so that we can adapt the message to his or her level of understanding.

4) **Visual contact** means that feelings, not just words, will participate in the communication and thus **make the message clearer.**

5) **Our opinions should be explained respectfully.** This is a question of inviting and inspiring the other person with our message.

I wasn't aware of what a mistake I'd made until I saw the two takes months afterwards, sitting in a California studio with the air-conditioning full on. Were they trying to simulate the cold we felt at the time we did the takes?

Thanks to this project and to my constant visits to the United States, I caught some of the worst colds of my life. I discovered that Americans love to have their air-conditioning on full blast. I also got tired of hearing a sentence which, if Twitter had existed back then, would have become a trending topic:

#you'vebeenupEverestsoyoucan'tfeelcold.

Anyway, it was in that studio that I realized what had happened up there, three months earlier. The first take wasn't good. In fact, it was pretty pathetic. I had exited the shot and had completely wasted David and Roberts' framing.

The second take was, in aesthetic terms, far more successful, being a direct line that took in all the beauty of the ridge, with the impressive image of Makalu, the fifth highest peak in the world, in the background. That image would end up being the one on the poster and the DVD.

One reason for the squabble we'd had was because we were carrying only just enough film and batteries for the required takes. I had wasted precious minutes and we didn't have any extra rolls of film.

Giving in to the circumstances

We keep on climbing. For quite a long stretch, the edge of the ridge is wide and fairly safe. There are no fixed ropes. In fact there haven't been during the whole ascent, which is something I like. It gives me more of a feeling of justice, of being fair to the mountain.

My inner struggle not to use oxygen – I was ordered to do so at the last minute – is a battle to the end. This is one of the issues that I dwell on during the long ascent.

We can't always do things the way we want to. Up until now, I've been doing pretty well. On previous expeditions, I'd climbed in a way that I consider to be suitable for mountains. I never climbed with Sherpas and much less with oxygen.

I accepted this project on the condition that I wouldn't be bringing any oxygen bottles. I understood and accepted the necessity of using Sherpas for the equipment they would have to carry, what with a heavy 24 kilo camera, the 12-kilo tripod, the lenses that weighed between one and two kilos each, and batteries weighing around three kilos.

We had to accept help from the Sherpas, because on the day of the summit we would be carrying nothing but our own gear, just as we did during the entire expedition.

THE MIND IS A PARACHUTE

I have never been on an expedition on which everything went absolutely according to plan. There's always something you have to change, or a situation to which you have to adapt. You have to be flexible, and in order for the project as a whole to be a success, we all have to **make some concessions, which should not be confused with giving in.**

There's no need to get dramatic. The world isn't coming to an end, we simply have to change our single-minded way of seeing things. We need to realize that there can be many parallel realities, as it were, and that they're all good if they can be of use in order to achieve our goal.

Albert Einstein said that **"the mind is a parachute; it only works when it's open".** When we cling to preconceived ideas, we think rigidly and can't adapt to change. Whether we are on an expedition to Everest or facing any situation which is difficult or risky, we need to open our minds and be flexible. To accept alternatives and solutions which we hadn't even been able to imagine.

Especially when the going gets really tough and everything seems impossible.

I had to adapt at the last moment, David told me I would have to start climbing with oxygen. Our pact had changed after the tragedy that had taken place on the mountain ten days earlier. Fifteen deaths in the course of a single expedition: the worst disaster in the history of Everest. That and the tiredness we felt after making the rescue, changed the rules of the game.

The director of the IMAX documentary didn't want to take any unnecessary risks by letting me make the ascent without oxygen. On the one hand, I wouldn't be able to keep up with the rest of the group. I'd be slower. In other circumstances, they would have waited to do the filming, but after what had happened, the group was in a state of extreme nervous tension.

David needed me on the summit and in the film. It wouldn't have made any sense at all for them to have been up there, filming some stunning scenery, but without anyone appearing in the images.

I understood all this perfectly well, I accepted it and took it on board, even though, all of a sudden, I lost my personal motivation.

MAKING LEMONADE

An old saying goes "**If life gives you lemons, just make lemonade.**" In the days leading up to the assault on the summit of Everest I had to find a way of feeling comfortable with a situation that had gone sour for me. My reason for being here was to climb Everest without oxygen, and I knew that wasn't going to happen. I needed to get my motivation back precisely at this most delicate of moments.

Not knowing why you're doing what you're doing, not having a good reason, a sincere, genuine objective, can destroy your motivation. And motivation is the motor behind all our actions. Without it, we wouldn't get anything done.

I found a new incentive in the documentary itself, in the film project that were working on. I discovered that it was also exciting to make history with something that nobody had so far managed to do: to film in the IMAX format, dragging that huge, heavy camera up the summit of Everest.

Once we understand that things don't always work out the way we want them to, we have to squeeze as much as we can out of what life gives us - and enjoy the lemonade.

The half-empty bottle

When we reach a height that we reckon is more or less halfway to the top, we mark a reference point. We make it as visible as possible, just in case we don't get a good view of it on the way down, either because it's covered by foggy clouds or because, due to some problem or other, we have to make the descent at night. At this point, we leave one of the two oxygen bottles that each of us is carrying on the snow, even though it's half full.

From this point on, we'll use a new one, in order to get to the summit and come back down to where we've left the used bottles. Which we'll then pick up and use to make the descent down to Camp IV.

It simply doesn't occur to me that, due to an oversight, I'll make the entire descent from the summit without oxygen.

Our whole expedition is hanging by a thread. After having rushed to help in the rescue ten days earlier, we've used up a lot of our material, including the most important and valuable part of it: the oxygen.

It's not as if we have so much of it that we can afford to leave deposits all over the place, with the result that we don't need so many porters. Each person carries his own bottles, which are relatively small, which means we have to limit our oxygen supply. The flow is usually that of two or three liters per minute. There are some people who set it at four liters per minute – that's the standard measuring unit – but I'm using a flow of half a litre per minute. That's very low, but enough to make a difference and get me to the summit.

On this expedition, I'm enjoying the strategies we have to employ, like the one used for the oxygen. We decide what needs to be done on the spur of the moment, where we're going to place the material, who's going to climb first or later, how to distribute the tents and which turns we'll take to acclimatize ourselves. We're studying how best to exploit our resources as best we can, especially now that we're facing the definitive assault on the summit and we're low on resources.

It's like a game of chess.

The art of strategy

I learnt to play chess when I was very little. Perhaps eight years old. My elder brother, Xavi, taught me. When it was raining outside, I sat with him in front of the balcony, between my mother's sewing machine and her varnished yellow table with its half rusted aluminum legs. It was untidy, covered with transistors, resistors, a soldering iron, solder, a radio ham's transmitter and QSL cards from around the world, pinned to the wall.

Those cards were the first thing that got me imagining what it must be like to travel and ever since then the smell of solder brings back the memory of that autumn and that corner in which I sat, daydreaming.

We played a lot of chess, or that's how I remember it. For a child of eight or nine, time stretches out longer than does when you're an adult. A year can seem an eternity. Twenty games can seem like half a lifetime.

He always won. He was five years older, but was patient enough to play with me.

Little by little, our games began to get longer and more complex. From starting and ending in three moves, we went on to making many more, with longer pauses between moves so we could think out several more ahead.

I loved that: to think of the moves I'd make after various pieces had already been moved. It was like guiding your own destiny through your own actions. And if at some point things didn't come out the way you wanted, which was almost always the case, then you'd have to think out a new gambit and once again look ahead at the moves you'd make.

The piece I liked the best was the knight. It's the most unpredictable, the most elegant, the one which is least tied down. It can lurk behind a hidden gambit and make moves that even the queen isn't allowed to do.

The day came when I beat Xavi, and that was the last time I played with him.

Two decades later, Everest was the great chessboard, and each one of us was a piece that had to be moved with care. Even the simplest pawn could win or lose the game.

One step at a time

Snow is hardest where the wind blows and is easier to walk on, but you can't always use its consistency as a guide, because it can lead you to the edge of a precipice.

David and I link up once we leave the windy ridge and head for the inside of the slope.

I've spotted a section with fixed ropes and think that if we take hold of them we'll move a little faster, with less effort. David takes hold of one and it comes off loose in his hand.

We move forward, up to our waists in snow. It's crumbly and soft and it's a real effort to climb. Every step we take feels as if we're moving backwards. I lose track of how long we've been doing this. It's the toughest physical battle I've yet had with the mountain and it leaves me exhausted.

Up until now, when climbing I felt happy and optimistic because of how fit I was. From this point on, however, I can feel every step I take. When I look up, I see the summit of the ridge and, when I finally reach the top, instead of a clear view of where I'm headed, I see another ridge with another summit. And this goes on countless times, to the extent that it gradually wears down my patience.

I decide to do something which I've found very useful when I'm tired: counting my steps. First from one to ten and, when I've done that ten times and have reached a hundred, I decide whether to take a break or not. If I see that I can go on without stopping, I go up to 200.

It's extremely important to take as long as possible before taking the first break, because there's usually no going back. If you take your first break after two hundred steps, you'll find it difficult to take the next one after three hundred.

THE POWER OF CONCENTRATION

Counting keeps my mind off my tiredness. In a highly demanding or risky situation we can't let ourselves think about fatigue. In my case, counting prevents me from making silent complaints such as "I can't go on, I want to stop, I'm in pain". A number simply takes me to the next number and to the next step. And then another...and yet another. And so on up to the end.

This is nothing but a form of **meditation, a conscious, active and alert mental state in which your mind doesn't think about anything and so you don't get anxious dwelling on how far away everything is, or on how worn out, tired or ill you feel.**

Concentrating on one single thing, be it walking, or peeling potatoes, the way Zen monks do, **allows us to channel all our energies in one direction and achieve excellence.**

As opposed to the great waste caused by mental dispersion, it's a matter of **doing one thing only at a time.** If we do it well, the phantoms of fear, stress and concern will disappear.

A dangerous communication breakdown

This is how I get to the South Summit, at 8,750 meters. There is a small rise, just in front of the final stretch which leads to Everest's highest point. It's a short distance, but takes a long time. From here I can see the whole route almost up to the summit.

A couple of the porters and David are already there.

I sit down nearby for a rest. We end up waiting for quite a while and I don't understand why we haven't got going again. Then I realize that one of the porters has turned up without a rucksack. He wasn't feeling very well, and was moving very slowly with that load on his back.

Logically enough, he reckoned that without the rucksack he would speed up, and that is in effect the case, but it's no use to us if he makes the ascent and a part of the camera doesn't. Each and every one of the rucksacks is essential for setting up that machine and filming at the summit.

For a porter, and especially for a Sherpa, reaching the summit of Everest confers great prestige, that will give him status and renown in his village and community. It represents an opportunity to get a more advantageous job which is less dangerous and better paid. In his case, between this job and him, there was a missing rucksack.

I then realize that we've missed a very important detail: each and every member of the expedition - mountaineers, porters, cooks, everyone - needs to know exactly what the aim of the expedition is.

At first sight, it looks as if our aim is to reach the summit of Everest, but in fact, that isn't the case. Our main objective is to get the IMAX camera to the summit, with at least one person who can operate it, and, if possible, to get some of the actor-mountaineers in the shots. Even if the latter weren't possible, we could still consider it a success.

Sometimes, objectives can seem very obvious, but a lack of communication can make us lose sight of them. Which is why, in high risk situations, it's important to clarify repeatedly what it is we want and how we want to do it.

For a few hours, a little mistake like this one almost ruined not only our three months of hard effort, but also the years of work spent on the technical preparation of the camera and the team.

In a single day, there had already been two misunderstandings.

The afternoon of the tragedy

Jangbu Sherpa puts down his load and goes off to look for the rucksack which his colleague has abandoned.

From the South Summit you have to make a short descent to the other side. Then you go up to the ridge of the arête, which often has cornices, and that will lead you to the famous Hillary Step, and, finally, to the summit of Everest.

I look out of the corner of my eye at the summit and the Step, but the part which bothers me the most is just underneath me, seven meters below, where Rob Hall lay.

Rob died eleven days ago. That was on May 10th, when, together with two other expeditions, he went up to the summit to guide a group of clients. It was more or less here that what has become known as the 'Tragedy of '96' started, which since then has become an important chapter in the history of Everest.

After the build-up of people that took place that same day on the summit, in which the majority were clients of two commercial expeditions, and one non-commercial one which was, however, guided by Sherpas, Rob ended up coming down from the summit too late. He did it at four in the afternoon, very tired and in the middle of a storm. He was accompanying one of his clients, Doug, who collapsed during the descent, just a little way above the Hillary Step.

He was the last client, and Rob stayed with him and tried to help him. At two in the morning, already without oxygen, he was still trying to get him out of there.

We'll never know exactly what happened to Doug: whether he fell, or died of hypothermia, or if he managed to come down the Step. We only know that at five in the morning, Rob managed to drag him to the foot of the South Summit. There he established radio contact with us and with his wife, who was in New Zealand and seven months pregnant.

The little communication we had with him made our hair stand on end. He was begging for help which, up there, in the middle of the storm, nobody could give him. Ed, a great friend of his, did everything possible to make him get up and climb those final seven meters to then try, if necessary, to slide down the slope.

We managed to get hold of a couple of Sherpas who, exhausted though they were from their efforts the day before, left Camp IV to look for him, but after a short while they turned back because of the bad weather.

We heard him say his last words, in the middle of the storm, as he talked to his wife who was pregnant with their first child. After that, nothing. He was so high up that nobody was able to help him. Eight people died during those few days.

DIFFERENT VIEWS OF THE TRAGEDY

This whole story would later be told in detail by Jon Krakauer in his book *Into Thin Air*. I've heard that it's a brilliantly told story and so it must be, given that it became a worldwide best-seller. I didn't want to read it when it came out. Maybe I'll do so now that time has passed and I can look at everything from a different perspective.

It was enough for me to live through everything that happened, both during and above all after the expedition, when several critics laid into the people who were on the mountain that day with comments that were both gratuitous and generalizing. Such criticisms were often made by people who had never gone out for a walk longer than an hour in their entire lives, but they had the temerity to make judgements about what was right and what was wrong up there on the mountain.

Not even those of us who have breathed the rarefied air at those heights, those of us who know just how exhausted the body, the soul and one's reasoning can get, would dare to judge whether it was wise for Anatoli (one of the guides) to climb without oxygen if there were going to be so many people up there, nor could we make a judgement concerning many other matters that cropped up during those forty-eight hours.

Should anybody be curious about these particular events, I would recommend they read two books, in order to be fair to both sides. That of Jon Krakauer and also the book which Anatoli's partner, Linda Wylie, wrote after he died a year later on Annapurna. It's called *Above the louds* and hasn't been translated into either Catalan or Spanish.

I have my own memories of the expedition, as well as my diary. I usually write one on every trip I make. Sometimes they're full of details and at others they're more superficial. At all events, I never look at these journals again once I've returned home. But the one made during that expedition is different. I actually have looked at it two or three times. And every time a colleague on my expedition has written a book, I have felt it necessary to read it so as to compare it with my own memories. The books are *High xposure*, by David Breashe *No hortcuts to the summit* by Ed Viesturs and *Touching my ather's oul* by Jamling Norgay.

I've realized that we each have our own reality, with small variations and subtleties which reveal the way we understand the world.

Ropes up to the summit

I poke my head over the edge and see the body of Rob Hall, almost completely covered by the snow under the cornice. I pull my head back at once and feel a terrible sorrow, a sadness which causes a knot in the pit of my stomach. I also think about Ed, who has just passed close by him, and about the effort he made on that fateful day to try to get him to stand up.

I'm walking fast because the path is downhill, I barely look at Rob, although I can't help thinking about him all the time. Once again, I try to make an effort to think about something else.

That's not so difficult for me, because when I get to the Hillary Step, a twelve meter stretch of rock and ice, I realize I'll need to concentrate as much as possible.

It's really not that hard. If we could climb down it at sea level, it would involve a bit of rock climbing without ropes, or a course for first-timers. The problem is that up here the snow is dry and loose and there is hard ice in the fissures. That problem is combined with the limited freedom of movement caused by our boots and down suits, as well as the tangle of ropes which has piled up on this final stretch. There are old ones, new ones, broken ones and frayed ones. Everything together makes things a lot more difficult than they normally would be.

Once we reach the tangle of fixed ropes, I take my ascender[1] and choose the rope I'm going to use. For greater safety, I hook a safety hook carabiner to a group of four or five more ropes.

Once I've climbed the first five meters, I sit on a small ledge to change the rope ascender. The safety hook carabiner has got caught up in a mass of twisted ropes. I'm busy with all this when I notice something sliding around my mouth. All of a sudden, I recognize the taste of iron. My nose is bleeding.

The memory of blood

Up until now I hadn't thought about anything other than the technical aspect of each movement. But the taste of iron, like different smells, can take you back in time and space, awakening a tiny split-second recollection which grows and grows until you end up living out years of your past life.

I must have been very little, because I remember waking up in a barred wooden crib in the room, I shared with my three brothers and sisters. In 1976, my grandmother was still alive, because I wouldn't move into her bedroom until she died, when I must have been about four or five.

One morning, upon waking and opening my eyes, the part of the sheet that was under my face was stained red with dried blood. I have a very clear memory of how, the night before, something humid had flowed out of my nose, just like now, and how I'd wiped my face with the sheets.

---

[1] Self-locking safety locking device. A mechanism with a cam that is attached to the rope which allows you to slide up the rope but not down.

I woke up and cried when I was little, but not now, at 8,700 meters. I was scared out of my wits and from then on couldn't stand the sight of blood. It was an irrational, infantile fear, to the extent that if I saw anyone bleeding, that person too threw me into a panic and I would keep well away, for good.

That happened with a child at nursery school. I remember it was winter, because when I think about it I can smell the smoke from the chimneys and remember the weather was foggy. We were in the playground and I was playing at going up and down some old semi-circular bridges - made out of metal tubes and painted in different colors - without using my hands. Suddenly, I saw one of the children fall backwards off a swing, banging his head against the gravel. A stream of blood ran down the back of his neck and stained the back of the black and white striped smock that we all wore back then. They took him away. I knew that when they took you away, it boded no good.

From that day on, every time I saw that child, I got frightened and moved away or even ran off.

Conquering fears

There are fears which you overcome without really knowing how, as was my case with my fear of blood. There are other times, however, when you remember perfectly well how you managed to get rid of such an absurd phobia.

I'll never forget how I stopped being afraid of the dark. Although I was already fifteen, I hadn't intended to face up to this fear consciously, but I had to do just that because this fear was an obstacle between me and my wish to go potholing. A whole world of explorations, journeys and friendship opened up before me. In the end my wishes, my longing for adventure and my emotions proved stronger than the fear

Every time I lowered myself into a chasm, the darkness and my demons were waiting for me inside. But with time, I managed to forget that I'd once been afraid.

THE BEST POSSIBLE VICTORY

The wish to do something is the best impulse when it comes to breaking such mental limits, be they large or small, which often stop us in our tracks and hold us in check.

Few things give greater satisfaction than managing to take the step forward that you thought you were incapable of, no matter how small it might be. Conquering one's own fears is a powerful source of self-esteem which gives you the necessary confidence in order to overcome the next obstacle which life or your own mind has in store for you.

There is a Chinese proverb which says: **"If one man overcomes a thousand warriors in battle and another man overcomes himself, the latter is the stronger of the two"**.

We should not be afraid to go to war with those thoughts which limit us. We should not be afraid of being afraid. Anything which causes fear is an invitation from life to outdo ourselves and to climb a little higher, on our own mental Everest.

Those years of initiation in potholing, apart from helping me handle the ascender more skillfully, were also one of the most important periods of enrichment and discovery in my life.

Oddly enough, at 8,700 meters I'm using the same ascender as I was back then. And I'm not trying to break any records by seeing how long this particular article will last. It's simply that this is the ascender I happened to have had at home. Its old metal cogs have been worn down by mud and thousands of meters on the clock. Which is why here, from to time, when the rope gets some snow on it or is frozen, it slips a little and gives me a bit of a fright. It's as if this old friend on so many expeditions were trying to tell me: "Hey, don't trust me too much; we're not that good; it's impossible for us to be completely safe."

Many years ago, I went down with it into total darkness. I was seventeen and was taking part in a campaign – as potholing expeditions are called - into the GESM chasm, 1,070 meters underground, in Malaga. Now, paradoxically, it's taking me up to the highest point on the planet, to seek clarity, to touch the light.

The relativity of time

As soon as I manage to undo the tangle of knots, ropes and stained handkerchiefs, I come back from the past to the present moment.

I stand up with an effort and keep on walking slowly uphill. Followed by Jamling.

Seeing that there isn't any wind, and that we are getting closer with each step, I find myself becoming more thrilled and motivated. I feel happier and happier. This very excitement makes everything seem to take ages. I want to get there as soon as possible. I feel as if time is moving very slowly, although that's impossible: indeed. the reverse is true.

According to Einstein's theory of relativity, the lower the altitude, the slower the passage of time, because we are closer to the Earth's gravitational pull. The stronger the force of gravity, the slower times passes. So the more we distance ourselves from the gravitational pull, the faster time will pass and the quicker we will age. The difference is three microseconds per kilometer and year. That is to say, if Jamling's father, a Sherpa like himself, had decided to stay on the summit of Everest when he climbed up there in 1953, he would now be 0.0015 seconds older.

Thus, at least in theory, time passes faster up here, not more slowly.

The longest hundred meters of my life

My impatience has me making one of those fatuous questions that people often ask:

"Is it much further?"

And Jamling answers:

"I don't know. This is the first time I've been here."

We will end up laughing about this remark back at Base Camp.

Not much longer after this silly question, Ed appears. He's coming down from the summit. He's been waiting for us for quite a while and is getting cold, so has decided to begin his descent.

I'm happy, but in a reserved kind of way. Everything's going fine and the weather's holding, even though clouds are gathering in the valley. It's still early.

Ed has also climbed down to say goodbye quietly to his friends: Rob, Scott and the others. After giving me a hug, he tells me it's only going to take fifteen minutes. In fact, there are a hundred meters left, but they'll turn out to be the longest hundred meters of my life.

Given my nervousness, I go back to my mantra: ten more steps, and when that's done, ten steps more.

After so many hours of effort, of sleepless days and without eating barely anything, poorly hydrated and walking without pause, to think that you can make it up there painlessly, no matter how much training you've done, is a mistake. There comes a moment when you can't go on; you know it's going to happen. The only thing that'll keep you going is mental energy, conviction and techniques to deceive your tiredness.

So it is that, by pretending to deceive ourselves, we get to the top.

And now what?

It's possible to feel a bit disappointed when you reach the summit. Even Everest's. You've made such an effort, you've dreamed so much about it, you've prepared everything and you've imagined it so many times that, once you're there, you ask yourself: "Is that it? Isn't there anything else? No fanfares? Not even a little confetti?"

The effect of the summit is like being injected with a slow-working drug. When you reach it, often nothing happens. You're simply in a place from which you can't climb upwards any further. But, as the minutes, days and even weeks pass, the toxin you've injected yourself with up there starts to take effect until it leaves you in an exceptional state of spiritual and emotional excitement and lucidity.

It's half past eleven in the morning. It's taken us nearly twelve hours to climb the last 900 meters to the summit.

Before celebrating it with the others, the first thing I do, my chest on the snow, is lean over the cornice which leads to the North Face. It has a magnetic effect on me. This is one of the things with which I'd deceived my tiredness as I climbed. I was dying to see this side of the mountain, to see from above how the precipice falls away.

From up there, however, the slope isn't as steep as I'd thought. You can't really see the precipice or the verticality of the Hornbein Couloir, the route on the other side which we'd had a go at a few months ago earlier in the purest Alpine style: not a single fixed rope, no porters, no pre-established camps and no oxygen.

Xavi Lamas

The clouds break and for an instant I catch sight of the Chang Zheng Peak. Xavi Lamas has been lying underneath it for the last nine months. I cried my eyes out back then, but I refuse to do so this time round. Instead of shutting myself away with such sad thoughts, I thank him, because he was part of the reason why I am here today.

Xavi was, first and foremost, a mountaineer, and he was also the doctor on our last two expeditions. I remember him as being short and slight, smart and sarcastic, and sharp-witted whenever he made any jokes, comments or observations. He was always up for a laugh. And he was very convincing.

I don't know how, but once he managed to get me to go to his place to massage his legs after he'd been running in a marathon, with the excuse that I was studying physiotherapy. I had to change twice on the metro. When I got back home that night, tired, I thought: "Wait a minute, wouldn't it have been more logical for him to have come here for the massage? After all, it didn't cost him a cent." In exchange, however, a few months later he sold me his second-hand mountain bike at a rock bottom price.

On that first expedition to Everest, I fell ill as soon as I arrived in Kathmandu. An attack of 'flu by way of a welcome. Xavi didn't think it mattered.

After a couple of days in bed, already half recovered and with all the bureaucratic paperwork completed, we headed off to the mountain. After a few days travelling by bus and truck we were dropped off at the Chinese Base Camp on the North Side of Everest.

But I wasn't getting any better. On the contrary, I was getting quite a lot worse. And now Xavi did look after me, to the extent that he stayed with me while the rest of the team went on ahead to set up the base camp.

It was a very small expedition. We didn't have two or three cooks, like other expeditions, nor did we have kitchens with all the usual utensils, so Xavi and Ernest made a deal with a very weird guy – he'd just climbed the North Ridge on his own – who said he would put us up in his tent until I made a full recovery, until it was time for him to go off and set up his own base camp.

I hardly saw him. I spent my days in my sleeping bag, sweating out the fever. But I do remember that he was involved in a strange incident involving some socks and the Tibetans who had stolen them.

When I was more or less OK, the three of us set off together. Xavi, who was on a doctor's grant from MIT in Boston, and the American – oddly enough, they lived in the same city – were chatting away.

I went on as best I could. Halfway up we separated, as the other guy's base camp was a day's walk away from ours.

A couple of days after our arrival, my fellow team members weren't about to make any concessions, and we set off to climb to the first acclimatization summit. According to alpine rules, you don't ascend and descend the mountain that is your objective by the same route, but rather you acclimatize yourself to the surrounding peaks and then, when you're ready, you launch the definitive assault.

As each person has different concerns and methods, there were people who wanted to climb half way up and sleep there, and then get to the peak in the morning, and others who preferred to leave later and do the ascent in one go.

Xavi, Manel and Ferran went off to sleep on the col. Ernest, Albert, Néstor, Gigi and I would head off in the early morning. We preferred to do the climb in one go. All eight of us would meet up on the summit, with just a few hours' difference between us.

Everything was going well. We reached the col where the tents where and Ricard, a colleague who had done a lot of trekking and had climbed up to this spot, came out to greet us. We drank a little tea and then went on, following the tracks of the three musketeers who had blazed the trail.

We'd gone a hundred meters and still had two hundred to go before reaching the summit, when, coming from above, we saw Xavi first, and, behind him, Ferran and Manel.

Xavi was perfectly happy, when suddenly a huge crack opened beneath his feet. I heard the dull thud of falling snow and the felt my heart go silent.

Ernest, who was just in front of me, yelled:

"Stick your ice axe in!"

Immediately, he crouched down to take the brunt of the wave of unstoppable wet snow that was rolling towards us.

Xavi had disappeared, swallowed up, and I stared incredulously at the avalanche coming our way.

All of a sudden, a little ridge of stones which marked a slender gorge diverted the avalanche in the direction of a large channel. It would come to an end 900 meters below us and we knew that there was nothing we could do.

It was a long, silent, dark, blurred, difficult, painful and absurd day.

Over the following days we went to sleep hoping that when not awake we would have a little time free of pain. We would wake up longing for it all to have been just a dream. At terrible moments such as this, you'd like to believe in magic, believe that someone might appear whose powers could change the course of events.

But we couldn't change a thing. Even if we'd sold our souls to the devil in order to have prevented everything from happening, facts were facts. They say that people don't die until they're forgotten, and none of us who were with Xavi have ever forgotten him.

The map of coincidences

After a few days, the American who'd put us up in his tent when I fell ill, turned up at our base camp. He'd decided to give up his ascent, after suffering an avalanche that had almost killed him.

He'd come to make a call from our satellite phone and to offer his condolences. This American was David.

Life ends up being a cluster of coincidences and crossings of paths. Sometimes we go back and find an acquaintance who will turn out to be important in our lives. If we were to draw a map with the people we know, if we examined where they have taken us and how certain coincidences run into each other, we would end up finding out that in this world we are all closer to each other than we think. Sometimes due to coincidence, and others to those opportunities which we take advantage of.

How different that expedition was from this one, and in some ways, how strange I feel to be up here now.

The clouds are thickening and I stop seeing Xavi, though in my head I can still hear a Pat Metheny song that he liked: *Always and Forever.*

Today, upon reaching the top, I haven't only tested the relativity of time, being as I am, in theory, on the one spot on the planet where it passes faster. But also my vision of the world, of my own priorities and motivations, have entered an orbit of constant relativization which I have no wish to relinquish.

The other half of the journey

Jamling and I give each other a big hug. For me, it's been an honor to climb this mountain with him and to reach the summit together.

He prays, talking briefly to his father, the first man to climb this mountain: Tenzing Norgay. From what he says, he has made the ascent only to feel closer to him.

Then, we film. We work for an hour, setting up and then dismantling the heaviest camera that's ever been brought up here. We take photos, we hug each other, we watch the approaching clouds. When we've finished, we begin the descent as the drug of the summit continues to take effect.

Sometime afterwards, I will think long and hard about what we achieved on that day.

But I don't want to spend much time talking about the summit. Many people might think of it as the most epic part of an expedition, the project's crowning moment. For me it is only the half-way point, and the other half deserves as much respect or more: the descent to Base Camp.

Once again, our objectives seem clear enough, but there can be mix-ups. The real peak isn't here, but at Base Camp. The final aim of the expedition is for all of us to celebrate it together, down there. If we aren't sure about this apparently obvious objective, we might make the mistake of not apportioning our stamina correctly. You can't burn yourself out during the ascent; you have to reserve part of your energy so as to make the descent properly.

A grave oversight

At around 12.30, we begin the descent. On my way down I feel extremely tired, something I attribute to the effort I need to make. When I get to the bottom of the South Summit and climb the small ramp in one go, once I'm at the top I collapse onto my knees on the snow, gasping.

Suddenly, I realize what's going on. For quite a while I've been on the move without any oxygen. I didn't shut it off during the long waits – on the Balcony, at the South Summit, on the final summit – and that is a serious mistake.

For someone who's using oxygen at altitude, even though, as in my case, it might be a minimum dosage, a cutting off of supply is like going at 60km per hour and then stopping short. For a human body, it's as if you were suddenly being strangled at the same time as a rucksack weighing 80 kilos were slung on your back. Each time you want to make an effort, you can't get enough air and your body feels heavy. On the other hand, if you stand still, you barely notice it. In fact, on the summit I spent a long time without the mask and it didn't make any difference.

I've got no choice: the only solution is to not lose concentration, to keep up a slow but constant pace. If I stop to gather strength, I'll have to make sure it's for a very short time.

I've got half a bottle waiting for me at the half-way depot. I've got through the toughest part, so I focus on how I can make the descent without ropes, safely, without any problems, until I get there.

I've had to sit down a couple of times. I count to thirty then get up. I can't allow myself any more time, because I don't know what might happen next.

The fright of my life

When I reach the depot, Jamling helps me to change the oxygen gauge, but makes a mistake and sets the regulator at three litres per minute.

I realise this a little further downhill, and stop to readjust it. When I've finished doing that and am calmly putting my rucksack back on, one of the porters passes by and says something to me, pointing to something on the ground, right next to me. I turn to see what he's talking about and when I look at it properly I get the fright of my life. It's the body of Scott Fisher, the guide on the commercial expedition who also died on that fateful night. I hadn't seen him thanks to his rucksack, which is half wrapped around him. His body is in a really strange position, probably from the effects of altitude, and his hand is sticking out in a grotesque position.

So that I don't stop and keep on walking – the Sherpas believe that seeing a dead body on the mountain brings extremely bad luck – the porter tells me:

—*This is nothing, just garbage, garbage...*

With my heart beating like crazy, I wonder whether I ought to turn the oxygen back up and get out of there as fast as I can.

I make short work of the stretch leading down to the South Col.

After so much time spent concentrating, perhaps I've finally relaxed. Having spent so much time making sure that everything's safe, I was sure that nothing would or could happen. It's almost four in the afternoon and there's no wind. The tents are still far away, but I can see them. And we're all heading downhill.

Where the snow comes to an end, I tread on a sheet of hard ice, and become alert again, but it's too late. My legs are in the air and my bottom is flying. After slipping, I hit the ground with a blow that hurts like hell. I slide a little way downhill, but immediately manage to sit up.

I look around. Phew! Nobody's seen me. Jamling was quite a way behind.

A discovery that comes too late

We reach the South Col one by one, a little spread out, each of us immersed in his or her own thoughts. I stay outside the tent for a bit, holding the cup of tea that Sumiyo's given me.

I let the sunlight caress my face, eager for warmth. Although it's still cold, I don't feel it. A very odd sensation.

Sumiyo didn't climb to the summit. Days ago, David decided that she couldn't go up there. Her presence, right next to me, makes me feel uncomfortable. Not because of her, because of me.

I realise that during this period of almost three months, I haven't been able to understand her or get to know her better. Nobody on this expedition has managed to strike up a friendship with her. When seen in perspective, the communication with her has been rather superficial, maybe because of the cultural differences between us and because of the way we behave. Towards the end of the expedition, when she realised that she wasn't going to form part of the team that would get to the summit, we often lost sight of her at Base Camp. She spent her time visiting other expeditions and when she was with us, it felt like it was only because she reckoned she ought to be.

I don't think anyone made a proper effort with her. We never talked about it during the expedition, even though everyone was thinking about it. That was a big mistake: to think that little details aren't important, that they'll work themselves out or that they won't affect us much.

Everything is important and everything can end up having an effect. I would have liked to return home knowing that she was a friend and not a stranger.

Personal inventory

The first thing I do when I enter the worn-looking tent is take off my boots. I check that all my toes are intact. I congratulate myself: I've used the right kind of socks. Wow, what a fabulous achievement! Half of me says I don't give a damn, but the fact is that it's things like this – the choice of socks –that have made it possible for all of us who set off today to have reached the summit and come back in one piece.

It's four in the afternoon and I've stopped carrying oxygen. I like knowing that I don't need it anymore and I decide to sleep without it.

The back of my neck hurts a lot. I've got a very small head and storm goggles are always too big for me. I didn't want to take them, afraid that the sunlight would destroy my retinas. A short time up there without goggles can make you blind for a good long while. The size of the storm goggles has made me spend the entire day in a really odd position, given that I had to stick my head out like a tortoise's to see where I was stepping.

My bum and right wrist have suffered a bit from my slip, but the rest is all in order.

Today, I've done a few little things badly; we all do that. It's impossible to be perfect. The difference lies in the demands of the environment. There are places where mistakes go unnoticed, but in others, such as this one, they can have disastrous consequences.

I've had enough proof of that today.

The day after

The following morning I get up in broad daylight. I hope that the tent'll warm up, but that isn't happening and isn't about to happen. How can it be that I'm not even sure where I am!

Getting dressed requires considerable effort. I'm more tired than I was the day before and I'd like to stay a while more in the sleeping bag.

I know that this camp isn't safe. Sitting still here is not going to improve things. We're at an altitude of 8,000 meters, in a tent. This isn't the Waikiki Hilton with room service. As a shelter, it's fine. It protects you and can save your life on occasion, but to stay here would only make things worse. Up here you burn up energy and wear yourself out. At 8,000 meters you'll never fully recover, no matter how still you are, or how little you do.

What's more, we have to go on filming. Things don't end at the summit, but when we manage to get back to Base Camp, 2,550 meters below us and twenty kilometers away.

Outside is Robert, David's assistant and the second cameraman, and a most tiresome person. This great Austrian mountaineer and I, haven't stopped joshing each other since we met, and he's kept a protective eye on me during the entire ascent. He thinks I haven't noticed. He's now telling me to come out, that we have to film something or other with the GPS.

When that's done, we start to climb down. I really want to. I want to start breathing a little more oxygen. I know that then I'll feel better and that the energy I've been losing will be replenished.

At first, my steps are heavy and slow, and I stop from time to time to get my breath back, but as time goes on I feel better. Above all, I make sure I don't stumble.

Something I'll never forget from that day is crossing paths with a South African expedition in the area known as the Yellow Band, due to its yellowish rocks, half way between Camps III and IV.

They were climbing up while I was climbing down. When I stopped in front of the leader of their expedition and said hello, without saying anything he unfastened my safety carabiner from the fixed rope. He then went on climbing, leaving me totally exposed to a serious fall.

What can you expect from people who, a few days earlier, refused to help during the rescue bid?

Surprised and shocked, I buckled up again and let out a torrent of abuse. I hadn't got annoyed with any of the people who've been on Everest this year, and this incident made me furious.

I go down all the way to Camp III and then down to Camp II in a bad mood, turning this incident over in my mind.

DEACTIVATING NEGATIVE LOOPS

Over time, I've realised what my mistake was: to allow that person to have the power to influence my mood. To waste my energy and my time.

That day, I should have climbed down feeling content, almost certainly tired, but happy to be making a safe descent. But instead of that, an individual whose existence was of little interest to me, took control of my thoughts during the three hours I needed to descend to Camp II.

What I should have done was to have made a mental note of the incident, no matter whether I was angry or not at that precise moment, to take suitable action if it were possible, and not to waste too much energy overall. Three hours, or even ten minutes of turning events over in my mind, is an absurd waste of time and effort.

Over the years I've learnt to control this kind of thing, some times better than at others. When something bothers me and I can't get it out of my head, if it isn't constructive and doesn't contribute anything, I cease to think about it. I do not allow this poison to stick around longer than it should. I close the door on it, and open another, very different one. I focus on a positive idea, be it a memory, a project or a wish. It's also useful to concentrate a lot on what you're doing at that given moment, like a mantra. Everything is useful, as long as it helps you to get rid of resentment, rage and bad temper.

The Hindu master Osho said that all you need is a breathing exercise to neutralise the negative mental loads which we sometimes hoard. He explained it as follows.

"Whenever you have a negative thought, breathe out immediately, as if you were getting rid of it through exhalation. Breathe out deeply, with the help of your stomach, and as you expel the air visualise how you rid yourself of the negativity. Then inhale deeply two or three times. Simply observe what is happening (...) Against negativity, begin by breathing out, not by breathing in. When you wish to absorb something, begin by inhaling; when you wish to get rid of something, begin by exhaling."

Gradually, everyone turns up at Camp II. Jamling is in a bad state. He has what is known as altitude blindness. On the day we reached the summit he took off his goggles and now he can barely see, mainly because of the pain caused by opening his eyes.

We have supper together, very tired and after two days of not eating anything. There is a contained happiness, a mixture of exhaustion and sadness at having to leave behind some colleagues who we will never see again.

A bit of drama

In the morning, when I get up, many of us are coughing and have dry throats. The blind are beginning to see.

Instead of going straight down to Base Camp, we stay here for a day. The weather is cloudy and bad and my feelings are a mix of relief, emptiness and coldness, as if I'd just got over the 'flu. But my thoughts are interrupted by David, who tells me we have to film.

I can't concentrate on the work 100%. I've given it my all these last few months and I'm exhausted.

David sticks the video camera in front of my face and asks me a question. I start to give my opinion in pretty bad English, having little energy to search for the right words and to put them in the right order.

In a harsh, brusque impatient tone, he tells me that that isn't what he asked me.

I don't know what he's asked me and to be honest right I don't really care. Tired and tearful, I answer in almost telegraphic language what I think he's asked me. These images were inserted into the film on a different timeline. In other words, they were filmed after reaching the summit, but in the film they appear beforehand.

I've always doubted whether David knew exactly what he was doing, taking advantage of my weakest moment, of extreme tiredness when my mind was worn out, so as to press the right button and get the exact level of drama and realism that the scene required.

As far as this scene is concerned, I've never known whether to call him a genius or an idiot.

Final conclusions

In the two days it took us to reach Base Camp, nobody has really got angry with anyone else. We've spent too much time together and we all know each other well enough to judge who intends to do what, and at what stage of tiredness everyone is, so we all cut each other plenty of slack.

Mentally speaking, we're feeling relaxed, because we've managed to do something that everyone told us was impossible: to take an IMAX camera to the summit of Everest, make a film, and come back down safe and sound.

Finally, on May 26th ten days after leaving Base Camp, with each of us facing up to his or her fears, we abandon Camp II to make the final descent.

We film a couple more scenes, including one in which we cross over another crevice. Where the hell does this damn perfectionist get all his energy from?

Towards the end of the morning, with the director's permission, we've been able to run off like kids at the end of a class, their homework finished

We don't come across anybody on the way. This route, which just a few weeks earlier had been full of porters and people on other expeditions, is now strangely quiet and lonely. Even the light has changed. It doesn't feel as if we're on the same mountain which we arrived at just a few months ago.

The glacier is sinking, changing its skin, and some of the safety ices stuck in the ice have been swallowed up, while others have been spat out. And now there's nobody who's going to pass by on a daily basis to repair them.

I feel as if I no longer belong to the mountain. Everything has its moment, and ours has passed. Much as we would like to keep everything around us just as it was two weeks ago, we have to accept that it's changed. Without looking back, I now have to worry about what lies ahead.

At Base Camp we are greeted with hugs, alcohol - just a little - and more food than we can eat. We need time in order to understand, process and accept everything that's happened.

That night, in the tent, in the sleeping bag, I curl up, my stomach shrinking. Now is the moment when I should close my eyes, unperturbed, but I'm too tired and emotional. I can't sleep. A thousand ideas and images are racing through my mind. I want to savour this moment, which is unique and unrepeatable.

I laugh with emotion, with enthusiasm, with satisfaction. I laugh even as I cry from pity, from nervousness, from knowing how lucky I am.

This week we achieved the unthinkable. We did it against all the odds, against all the strictures of common sense. Theoretically, we didn't have a chance, but we made the ascent. We took the camera up to the summit. We finished the documentary and we're in Base Camp, safe and sound.

I need some time to analyse how we did this. I need to put the pieces together and go back to the beginning to understand that every step we have taken on this journey and every person who has taken part in it, have been indispensable.

COMMITMENT, CONVICTION AND PASSION

There's something that I mulled over during the descent. In the beginning, I wasn't aware of it, but now that some time has passed, now that I can put this expedition into perspective, I've come to understand it: the importance of **commitment** and **conviction** when it comes to making a success of a project like this one.

A third vital ingredient is **passion: loving what you do.**

Everyone has given his or her all to ensure that this project would be the best of its kind in the world. We were convinced, we wanted to make a documentary that was unparalleled in the history of the cinema and of mountaineering.

There are many degrees of implication and commitment in any given task. We could have done the minimum necessary, enough so that nobody could find fault with us, but without sticking our necks out. But if things are done like that, one barely survives and sometimes not even that. At most, you'll achieve what many other people have. With that kind of attitude, you won't make any kind of difference.

When you really want to achieve something exceptional, the only way to do it is to put your body and soul into it.

That would explain why, for instance, David and Robert were often ready to get up hours before the rest of us to film a beautiful, icy rising sun, or to show how the moon lit up Base Camp. And all that after a long, exhausting day at sub-zero temperatures, even though they had other images which weren't as good but which would have been passable.

Ed had the same attitude, and took it upon himself to leave before everyone else to make a path in the snow to make things easier for those who followed.

Commitment, conviction and passion account for why the porters also went back to working for us after having done most of their work and after the tragedy, once again lugged the material we needed up to Camp IV, which had been used during the rescue, when quite possibly everybody simply wanted to go back home.

It was this same spirit that helped me reshoot that scene up there, at an altitude of 8,000 meters. Theoretically, we already had several images which, properly edited, would have been good enough for a more or less coherent documentary. But we didn't want a more or less coherent or more or less good documentary, we wanted the best documentary possible.

Commitment and conviction combined with passion make for an invincible cocktail. In my case, I grew passionate about the filming when we were on the mountain. I didn't belong to the world of film or of documentaries. I didn't have a clue as to what an **IMAX** camera was, before this expedition. But I knew that having enough energy to climb meant nothing if I didn't also have the patience to be filmed.

One of David's great skills, as the person in charge of the documentary, was to know how to transmit to others the passion he had for his work.

At a time as difficult as the one in which millions of people are living through nowadays, when everything leads one to get depressed or to throw in the towel, these three values have the ability to transform any situation, no matter how difficult.

—If we have **commitment**, we won't weaken and we'll never lose sight of the objectives we've set for ourselves, no matter how tough they might seem.

—If we have **conviction**, we can cope with all the difficulties, frightening moments and mistakes we come up against, precisely because we're convinced we will reach our goal.

—If we have **passion**, we will fight to make our dream come true, as if we were playing the most beautiful of games. Which, in fact, is exactly what we are doing.

A FEW STATISTICS ABOUT EVEREST

Base Camp: 5.400 m

Camp I: 5.950 m

Camp II: 6.500 m

Camp III: 7.300 m

Camp IV: 7.950 m

South Summit: 8750 m

Summit of Everest: 8.848 m

In the year of our expedition, 1996, the busiest day on the summit was May 10th, when 24 people reached it. That season, a total of 89 people reached the summit (counting both the Nepalese slope and the Tibetan one).

Between the 10th and 1th of May, 1996, eight people died on the mountain: five on the Nepalese slope and three on the Tibetan one. By the end of the season there had been a total of 12 deaths.

We all believed that after this tragedy, things would be different, that never again would there be such a large group on the mountain. We thought that not only the meteorological conditions would again be taken into account so badly, but that there would never again be such a large number of inexperienced and unskilled climbers.

In 2010, 170 people reached the summit on the same day.

The total number of people who reached the summit in 2013, was 6,208.

I did the 817th total ascent and was the 37th woman to reach the summit in the history of the mountain, and the first Catalan woman to do so.

II. A Beginning to End With.

We all have big changes in our lives that are more or less a second chance.

HARRISON FORD

I was running barefoot, on tiptoe, and still wearing my nightgown. I crossed the corridor of my still half-furnished apartment until I reached the fax machine. I hadn't slept much that night; I was a bundle of nerves.

Yesterday I'd told myself that I would sleep on the idea for a couple of days so as not to make a hasty decision, the way I usually do, but less than eight hours later I'd had enough of waiting and said yes.

Then came the worst part: waiting for an answer. I didn't know if David would still want me in on the project.

Almost three years earlier, in one of the most inhospitable parts of Tibet, on Everest's North Face, I'd met that thin, charismatic and attractive man. I wasn't exactly at my best at the time, but he could see that I was the right person for his project. Just before he left our Base Camp, he made a proposal: to form part of an international mountaineering team that would climb and film the ascent of Everest with an IMAX camera.

Aside from my ignorance of filming and the different formats involved, at that particular moment my mind was concentrated on what lay before me: a 2,500 metre wall of snow and ice. It was a straight line, graceful, without interruptions right up to the summit of Everest and it been climbed only a very few times: the Hornbein Couloir. I was determined to climb it in a few days in the purest alpine style.

Given the circumstances, my answer had been: "No, thank-you".

Rethinking life

We didn't reach the summit and in the autumn, I went back home. I was twenty-five, had recently completed a university degree course, I had a whole future to invent for myself and was in something of a hurry to make a decision. My grant had finished and I didn't want any help from the family. But Barcelona wasn't a cheap city.

Then I remembered David's proposal. It was a job that would pay my rent for a few months. It wasn't exactly the climbing style or the type of route that I liked doing, but I wasn't going to take it as a mountaineering challenge, but as a professional assignment.

I poked around in my expedition kit bag, still half unpacked, looking for the card I'd kept inside my diary. If it wasn't there, then I had a problem, given that I could barely remember his name. In those days, internet didn't have the mass of data it does now.

After giving an affirmative answer to David, I waited for a few days. As I began to see more and more possibilities in the project and became increasingly enthusiastic about it, the silence from the person who'd made the proposal made me think I'd been too late. I began to imagine a worst case scenario.

The art of waiting

And in the end he called me, but not to give me a definitive answer, as I'd expected. He told me that I had to do a screen test, which would take place in London. I would have to buy the ticket myself, and he'd reimburse me later.

I immediately began to imagine all kinds of things: what if the whole thing was a hoax... What if he'd invented it all? Sometimes, thanks to messages and bits and pieces that we force into a pattern that suits us, our minds put together a narrative which is coherent and credible, but false.

I wanted to weigh up all my options. I still had a fortnight if I decided to change my mind and end up not going. I went to check the ticket prices for the flight, and bought a ticket with my European Youth Card.

The die was cast.

In London, we met in park. David took out his video camera, and recorded while I answered a few questions in my broken English and that was that.

They'd be looking at this in California, he told me, and if the production team liked what they saw, they'd give me the job. I would have to wait some more, but at least now I knew that there was nothing else that I could do. So this time, waiting felt easier.

A friend from a modelling agency told me that not long ago they'd reported a group of people who'd rented some office premises so that they could make calls to modelling agencies. They asked for girls to be sent to them only so that they could see them in bikinis or lingerie in the course of false test shoots.

I was glad he told me that after I'd got back from London.

Preparations

We started the expedition very early. By the 8th of March we were already walking in Nepal, but we weren't heading for Everest.

David wanted to trek around the area with most of the team before starting the project properly. Like that, we'd get to know each other better.

One of the reasons why I'd rejected his initial proposal was that I didn't know anybody who was on this expedition. After my first experience in the Himalayas, which was a total disaster as far as getting along with each other was concerned, I decided that I didn't want to make the same mistake of finding myself on a mountain with a group of strangers. It was highly likely that at any given moment I would have to put my life in their hands or vice versa.

But there was one thing I hadn't counted on: David knew all of us.

EVERY SYMPHONY NEEDS AN ORCHESTRA

David chose mountaineers who he knew and who were technically prepared to meet this challenge, both that of climbing Everest and that of working on a documentary, and for him that was just as important as the fact that we needed to get along with each other.

In short, he hadn't brought together the best mountaineers in the world, but those with the best skills who would also work together best. Being the best in your field doesn't ensure any kind of success if you don't get along with the others. He put together a team of people who, in his opinion, would be able to work together successfully.

There are people who can tell what other people are like, how they are and how they might fit into a given group after only a short period of living together or with just a few hours of conversation with them. David had a very clear idea of what it was that he needed.

As the theologian H.E. Luccock said, "**No one can whistle a symphony. It takes an orchestra to play it.**" To use a musical simile, when it comes to the extreme challenge of making an IMAX film on Everest, there is no need for a Paganini who can show his virtuosity on a violin, but rather for a patient and well put together orchestra.

After the trekking, we got to work, familiarising ourselves with the camera, its use and assembly. And we started doing so at Kathmandu.

The working days were long. We often had to be up and about before dawn, sometimes to film the mist, the light or simply the stillness which is so unusual in a country as densely populated as Nepal. We often finished after dark, so as to take advantage of every minute of the light, colour and diversity that this abundant country provided us with throughout the day.

The training was exhausting, and prepared us for what was to come.

A mysterious box

The approach we took to Base Camp, passing through all the little villages as we gradually gained altitude, was longer than usual. We stopped more often than was customary at each step of the way, in order to follow the script.

In fact, the overall narrative was fairly simple: to go up to Everest, climb it with the camera and come back in one piece. The storyboard consisted of a series of basic images that David more or less had in mind, but we also improvised, depending on what we came across. As far as the text was concerned, nothing was written down. We didn't have to learn any dialogues, because the shoot was free of any kind of fiction.

I remember the Tingboche monastery very well, because we celebrated my twenty-sixth birthday there. Robert, the second cameraman, gave me a bar of chocolate.

It was snowing and the periods when I didn't have to work were getting boring. After a few days I'd come to enjoy taking part in the shoot, even if it was just a matter of, say, holding up the reflector so that Jamling could be properly lit.

The camera looked pretty impressive and different from all the other ones that had been taken to that part of the Himalayas so far. It wasn't the first day that the monks of Tingboche had seen film-makers at work. Even so, they approached us timidly, curious, gathering up the folds of their saffron coloured tunics as, amused, they whispered to each other.

One little lama who couldn't have been more than six years old walked around full of curiosity, clearly wanting to look through the viewfinder. David immediately stood to one side and let him take a peek. The child stood there for a while with his eyes glued to the viewfinder and his hands clasped, while we waited for his reaction. When he finally unstuck his cheek from the camera he was frowning unhappily, disappointed, something which stood out more because of his shaved head.

When he asked him what had happened, the boy replied the only thing he'd seen through that hole was what was on the other side of the camera. So we asked him what else he'd expected to see, and he answered that he'd hoped to see what was inside the camera, that sealed, mysterious black box that made so much noise.

That's why he'd looked down the hole.

THINKING OUTSIDE THE BOX

We often interpret our own reality as if it was the only one in existence, basing ourselves on our beliefs and what we've learnt from our experiences, on our vision of the world. But an artist doesn't see a mountain the way I see it, nor does a writer, or a doctor. Nor does a Sherpa like Jamling see a mountain the way I see it, and yet all these perceptions are equally real and valid.

Nobody is in possession of the truth, because we understand the world depending on who we are and what we have lived through. It requires a considerable effort to break free of everything that has conditioned us and to see a given situation from different points of view, like the Tibetan boy who looked through the camera's viewfinder.

"To think out of the box" is to **think beyond, not to look for obvious answers, but rather to go beyond that.** Thinking out of the box, for our little lama, meant wanting to know what was inside our mysterious box.

To help us think outside the box, Edward de Bono's classic book *Six Thinking Hats*, suggests a method for finding more creative visions and solutions: that we symbolically wear six hats which allow us to deal with any given subject in ways that are completely different, according to their colour::

* **White:** we will limit ourselves coldly to the information which we have, without making any subjective evaluation of it.

* **Red:** we will give our intuition free rein and listen to what it tells us.

* **Black**: we will take any possible risks into account and look at how we can deal with them.

* **Yellow**: we will focus positively on the value and benefits that can be derived from any given situation.

* **Green**: we will examine all alternatives and possibilities, no matter how strange they might seem.

* **Blue**: we will analyse the thinking – prejudices, preconceived ideas – which we use to focus on the matter in hand.

Base Camp

With some 200 yaks laden with all the material we needed in order to live for two months, on April 3rd, 1996, we reached Base Camp.

Up until then, all the expeditions I'd been on had used solitary base camps, where there were only a few people or no people at all. Here, on the other hand, there were a total of eleven expeditions. Some were small, with a single Westerner and his porters. Others, like those of Adventure Consultants or Mountain Madness, had twenty-something members each. Both of these were commercial expeditions.

Ours, even though we were there to carry out two tasks, climbing and filming, was relatively small: ten Westerners, of whom six were mountaineers and the others whose job was to do production related work at Base Camp.

Our group of back-up porters was also relatively small, given the extent of the project. It was made up of a fixed group of six Sherpas whose job was to carry the camera and all its components with us at all times. Twelve more Sherpas were there to administer supplies and manage the kitchen. One of the cooks, Norma, was an old acquaintance. This would be our third and last expedition together. Years later he would die in a helicopter accident in Nepal.

I calculated that at Base Camp, what with the expeditions to Everest, Lhotse and Pumori, there was a population of around five hundred people. For all these mountaineers, porters, back-up teams and visitors, a small improvised city had been built on the glacial moraine. The coloured tents, plastic pavilions and dry stone walls would all vanish three months later.

Our centre of operations was the spacious dining tent, with a varied assortment of food thanks to the work of Paula, the Base Camp Manager. There we always had something to pick at between meals, and different kinds of teas and infusions.

Communication was a vital element in ensuring the success of our expedition, which was made up of mountaineers and workers from many different cultures, with different idiosyncrasies and with very different ways of understanding the world. What was a superficial, unimportant detail for one person, could be offensive for another.

Jamling was Indian; Sumiyo, Japanese; Robert, Austrian; David, Ed, Paula, Liz and Brad, American; I was Catalan; the porters and cooks were Nepalese. We couldn't afford any misunderstandings, be they cultural or linguistic.

There was a moment, at the start of the project, when I felt somewhat bewildered. I still didn't feel I'd found my place. I was mentally and physically trained to take on fast challenges, intensive projects, that were technically difficult and fairly solitary.

The way we were about to start the assault on Everest was completely different in all respects. The difficulties lay not in the technicalities involved in the route and the climb, but in the combination of making the ascent and the film at the same time. That aside, given the crowds of people in Base Camp, there was the added difficulty of making our film without interference from the other expeditions.

We didn't have the mountain to ourselves, we had to share it. That often meant stopping a shoot so as to let people pass by, waiting for hours until they disappeared from the shot or hurrying things up before they appeared in it.

DIVIDE AND CONQUER

Instead of getting ahead of events and worrying about how I would manage to climb and descend, or about waiting around or repeating a scene at Camp III, all of which was still a few weeks off, I concentrated only on what was in front of me.

I divided this huge mountain into little pieces, and I made sure to eat each of these pieces one by one and little by little, without swallowing the lot in one go.

My first objective was to arrive at Camp I. I concentrated all my efforts on that and took into account the difficulties I would encounter. This was a small challenge which I saw as being reasonable and easy to meet.

And I did exactly the same with each camp. I only bothered with the next stage on the agenda once I'd dealt with the previous one. The sum total of the four camps that lay ahead of me, the four steps I had to go up, would place me close to the summit, from where I could take the final step when the time came.

When it comes to our daily lives, **our obligations and problems can devastate us if we look at them altogether,** but as soon as we start to cut them into pieces, like those of a cake, **when we deal with just one thing and only then move on to the next one, what had seemed impossible becomes possible.**

Like Julius Caesar said: "Divide and conquer".

The Icefall

To get to Camp I, it was necessary to overcome the first obstacle, one of the most legendary places on Everest: the Kumbu Icefall.

It is located in the central area of the Kumbu glacier, exactly where the ice tongue breaks into thousands of little pieces before reaching Base Camp, along a three kilometre stretch. It consists of a labyrinth of immense blocks of ice which have fallen and are leaning against each other, and which sometimes allow just enough light through to let you make out bubbles of oxygen trapped for thousands of years in that blue glass.

On some of the stretches, the snow, compacted into overlapping layers, allows you to see what must have been the different climatology of past centuries. It is a dangerous place, alive and in constant movement, especially when the temperatures are highest, at midday, and when they fall suddenly at sunset. It's better not to be there at those two moments of the day.

This constant shifting of the ice tongue meant that the route had to be kept in optimum condition. Every day, a team of Sherpas paid for by all the expeditions would move over the icefall, re-attaching ropes, ice screws, loose anchors and the metal ladders with which we could cross the crevasses.

Despite which, sometimes the fastest, simplest and most economical route – in terms of energy expenditure – would be made totally or partially impassable by the collapse of a section of the glacier, or by the opening of an uncrossable crevasse. In which case, we had no choice but to start from zero.

DEALING WITH CHANGES

There are places in which you simply have to adapt yourself to circumstances. Obviously, the mountain won't change the way it is because you want to climb it. To fight against it would be absurd. If you don't want to or can't adapt yourself, you should go back home. As the great Mexican mountaineer Héctor Ponce de León often says: "Look girl, either you acclimatise...or you meet your demise."

One of the things I most admire in a mountaineering colleague is his or her ability to adapt to circumstances, to the environment, to change, with a positive attitude. There is nothing more discouraging than to be accompanied by someone who complains, because apart from the fact that this doesn't contribute anything worthwhile, it damages the group's morale.

There are people who adapt themselves naturally and with no apparent effort. These are the ones who know two basic things: how and why.

* *They know "how" to do things.* These are people who never cease to explore, to search, and above all to learn, who try out new, innovative tools when faced with different situations.

* **They know the "why".** They know exactly why they are there and when the first tricky change or situation appears, they don't turn back. On the contrary, as Friedrich Nietzsche said: **"He who has a why to live can bear almost any how"**.

Such people see uncertainties, difficulties, and changes as an opportunity, and problems as stimulating obstacles to be overcome, knowing that this will require all their ability, an effort which will be rewarded by the satisfaction of discovering new things about the environment or about oneself.

In that case, why is there so much resistance to change?
Basically, this is due to fear of the unknown, of being unable to do something different, of losing face, of no longer being the best in a field with which you had been perfectly familiar.

Laziness and vanity play a part when it comes to resisting change. A change sometimes means recognising that we don't know it all, that things can be done better or in a different way.

So, why change? Well, as Héctor would say, because there is no alternative if you want to go on, and because change is satisfying. Every situation which demands that you adapt yourself and solve problems is offering you an opportunity to take a step upwards in your personal evolution.

We all got on very well together. We joked, laughed, helped each other out or did as we pleased, without having to give any explanations nor to look for any. Everyone felt respected as a member of the group, each with his or her own skills. Each member of the expedition had theirs, and that made us feel part of a special whole. As we had different mountaineering styles, we complemented each other and took full advantage of our diversity.

That gave us another big advantage: at each stage of the climb, the most suitable people could be put in the lead. In this way, aside from the practical advantages, three things were achieved: self-esteem, a piece of the project's cake, so to speak, and enough synergy to make the team form a compact whole.

THERE ARE NO MINOR ROLES

The fact that within any given project we each have our part to play, no matter how small, means that to some extent, the project is ours. We make it ours, it makes us feel proud, and it pushes us to commit ourselves to it more and more. A part of the whole has been put together because of us, for which reason we're not about to abandon it if the going gets tough. It isn't as if it were somebody else's project, which neither concerns or affects us.

Commitment isn't something money can buy, it comes with feeling part of the project, with each of us leading our particular section.

All teamwork depends on the bond generated by trust between the different members. These are bonds which narrow the distances between one another, and which make the team compact, stronger and much less likely to break up when facing difficulties.

When we get together with other colleagues to work on a common project, or even when we work in a company with its various hierarchies, it is worth remembering something that Stanislavsky used to say to his acting students: **"There are no small parts, only small actors"**.

The Valley of Silence

As the days went by, climbing and filming, we arrived at and set up Camp I. And the next objective was Camp II.

To get here, we passed by the legendary Valley if Silence. Oddly enough, it was quite the opposite of the icefall stretch that we'd just done. As its name suggests, it's a broad, large, still and relatively flat valley, full of tranquillity, where the wind drops to zero. When that happen the temperatures can go up to over 40º Celsius then fall to below zero if a cloud happens to pass over.

It's a deceptive stretch, because you barely notice there's a slope, but there is one: after four kilometers along the route, you gain 500 meters in altitude. It turns out to be a place that's easy to underestimate, which needs to be approached with a great deal of humility if you don't want your own arrogance to slap you down.

Located in the same valley, Camp II was pretty safe. There are no nearby crevasses. It was broad and flat enough and there were no avalanches close enough to be worth worrying about. Once you'd acclimatised yourself properly, you could settle in comfortably, to the extent that we even had a permanent cook there during the entire expedition. We ended up spending eighteen days there, out of a total of two months for the whole trip.

Well situated in strategic terms, Camp II made it possible for you to be relatively close to the highest camp of all, and offered a good place to wait until the weather was good enough to head for the summit. And, if you were still getting acclimatised, it was at a good enough height for you to survive during some time; having said which, you couldn't overstay your welcome, as the drawbacks would have outweighed the advantages.

All the logistics involved in the expedition had to be planned to the last detail: the food, the fuel to cook it, where you went to sleep and where you would leave a sleeping bag if, on the way back, you had to sleep in that camp or in one further down. It was a chess game I loved to play; if you made a bad move, you had less options when it came to reaching the summit.

What I remember best of the Valley of Silence, is everything but the tranquillity. I recall the wild, anarchic storms; the gusts of wind that could appear from just about anywhere; Robert yelling from the dining tent for help to keep it standing; and I, who didn't want to leave my down wrapper inside the protective shell of canvas and nylon rods, which bent under the wind until they touched my nose. That said, I knew that these rods would protect me forever and wouldn't leave me in the lurch no matter how strong the wind was. In the end, I got out in order to help.

For almost an hour, with the wind whipping at us, we held that flimsy, unergonomic and badly designed structure steady, with its aluminium poles, until the wind slackened a little. Then David came out with...I knew what he was going to say, I was beginning to see exactly what kind of director he was:

"This wind would be great for the film."

"Noooooo..." I wanted to yell, but instead I smiled and said:

"Oooh, what a good idea."

I was beginning to learn how to act.

Robert was cut from the same cloth as his boss; they were like the Thompson twins.

We stood there for quite a while, filming that hurricane while we resisted the pummelling of the wind. It was so strong that we had to place a large rock over the camera so it didn't fly off: a piece of equipment what weighed all of 24 kilos.

And the worse thing of all was that David and Robert were smiling...Maybe I should have started to worry.

THE TWO KEYS TO PROACTIVENESS

It is only with genuine passion for what you are doing that you'll be able to cope with obstacles, and forget the blows and the exhaustion. In the case of these two, David and Robert, they not only went about their chosen task with passion, but they also had a proactive attitude that I had only seen before on very rare occasions.

They didn't wait around to hear what the head office in the United States said would be suitable for the documentary, but rather took advantage of any opportunities that came their way, no matter how tough they were, or they even created such opportunities so as to get the best possible results. They always took the initiative.

In his classic *The Seven Habits of Highly Effective Families,* Stephen Covey explains the two main attributes of proactive people:

1) *They act according to values that have been carefully selected and thought over:* many things can happen around them, but they are their own masters when it comes to dealing with these stimulae.

2) *They concentrate their efforts within the circle of influence:* they dedicate themselves to those things they can make something of. Their energy is positive, which is why they can widen their circle of influence.

Off to Camp III

I haven't yet explained, not wanting to go on for too long, that when we mountaineers reach a camp for the first time, we go back down to Base Camp, to rest, eat, sleep well, wash and replenish our material. We do not stay on the mountain for an indefinite length of time.

There's a formula we often use to acclimatise ourselves, which is applied at an altitude of up to just over 7,000 meters, which involves reaching the maximum altitude possible at the time, going back down to sleep, so that on the following day we will be able to sleep at a higher altitude.

So, after a few days at Camp II, having briefly reached Camp III, we went back up there to sleep.

Camp III was in the middle of the Lhotse Wall, on a slope of between 40º and 50º. It's an uncomfortable slope, whose old, hard ice barely allows you to drive the front spikes of your crampons into it. Whether you do that or whether you climb using the side of your feet, either of the two options ends up being irritating if you're not used to them.

The camp is made by hacking at the ice and building more or less flat platforms, taking advantage of the only spot where the slope is a little more gradual. It is not, however, by any means a terrace. The tents are set up on different step levels and placed between the fissures.

It's not exactly a comfortable place.

Ed put himself ahead of the group, on a slope 900 meters above us, determined to blaze a trail and release the ropes from a recent snowfall: we two were the first to make it that day.

When we got to Camp III, we started to cut out the platforms so as to pitch the tents we'd been carrying. We immediately put the sleeping bags inside.

It had been one of the longer days, and we'd all been lugging heavy loads, even though we'd been carrying the minimum necessary. I was pretty hungry that day, and was regretting not having brought more food. On the other hand, I couldn't have taken any more weight. Then Ed appeared with a tin of a Brie-like cheese, a delicacy which changed my mood completely. And not only that; it changed something else, without me being aware of it.

GENEROSITY IS CONTAGIOUS

Ed had made an act of generosity: he gave, without expecting anything in exchange. This was natural and frequent behaviour, coming from him, something which together with other traits in his character made him a born leader.

When, in a group, there's a generous person who offers, contributes, helps and gets involved, this attitude draws out other people's generosity, it makes you want to get involved too and offer whatever it is that you have. Ed's generosity stimulated that of the others, and strengthened the bonds between us more than ever.

Generosity is something often shown by people who are sure of themselves, people who are fully confident of their abilities and who are free of silly fears. As United States president Calvin Coolidge said, during the difficult decade of the 1920s: **"No person was ever honoured for what he received. Honor has been the reward for what he gave"**.

A tin of *brie*

There are three things in this world which bore me to tears, and I always avoid trying to have to do them if I can, using bribes, if necessary. One is ironing, and the other two are gathering up snow and melting it down into water.

At a high altitude, you need to drink more than at sea level. Not only because of the obvious dehydration due to physical effort, but also because up there the absolute humidity is zero. If to that we add that there are no streams to fill out water bottles, all the water being in a solid state, you can get the general idea. But things become even more complicated if to all that we add exhaustion and a lack of oxygen at 7,300 meters.

No sooner had Ed brought a tin of cheese to my tent, than, apart from it cheering me up no end, I felt I had to do something for him. He, too, was tired, just as much or more than the rest of us, after having marked the trail, released the ropes and having carried extra food without us knowing it, so I told him to go and get some rest, that I'd go out to gather snow.

There are places in which it's easier to do this than others, but in this dangling campsite nothing was easy. Even so, I took a rubbish bag, which is the best and lightest recipient for this job, and filled it with the cleanest snow I could find. Oddly enough, this time the work didn't bother me at all. I didn't feel the boredom I'd have felt if I'd had to do it just for me. Ed's actions didn't only affect one particular person, they had an impact on the whole group.

Giving up

Forty days after having arrived at Base Camp, after a few climbs up and down to and from the other camps, we were acclimatised and mentally prepared to launch our assault on the summit.

At Base Camp, we'd had meetings with the other expeditions so as to coordinate things between us. If we hadn't been filming, that probably wouldn't have been so necessary, but given that we would stop for quite a while half way up a slope in order to shoot, we didn't want to bother anybody and nor did we want the others to interfere with our filming.

We agreed that we would go up first, and that four expeditions would follow behind us, separated by one day's distance. In fact, that was to our advantage, because we would have to stage our scenes on the upper part of the mountain, from Camp IV up to the summit.

I spent a bad night at Camp III. The wind blew hard without any let-up and the snow piled up on one of the sides and collapsed the tent. No sooner had we got up than we weighed up the situation and decided this wasn't the right time to go to the summit. That meant that we couldn't wait around there for a day, because the other expeditions that were following would join up with us. So we had to go back down.

During the descent I said hello and wished luck almost automatically to the line of people who were climbing up using the fixed ropes. It was quite a crowd. Personally, I hardly knew anybody, but with Rob Hall – an experienced guide – we would joke around when we met. He had a habit, every time we ran across each other, of telling me ironically that the Pointe Walker of the Grandes Jurasses, a famous climb in the Alps which I'd done a few years ago, was easier than this.

"Go and try it yourself," I'd reply every time and he'd wink at me.

You need years of experience to know when not to doubt a decision, and back then I didn't have that much experience. As I climbed down, protected more and more by the bottom of the valley, the wind calmed down and the weather seemed serene and perfect. So why were we going back down?

Some of the mountaineers with whose paths we crossed asked us the same question: "Why are you going down, if the weather's good?" I myself thought for a moment: "What are we doing? We're losing a chance to get to the summit!"

THE POWER OF INTUITION

Too often we forget about our first reaction, which is the most instinctive and is often the right one. It tends to be a decision that our brain makes faster than we do, by looking at the fine points and analysing a series of variable factors without us realising it.

Over the years, you come to realise that the first decision is usually the best one, sometimes too when it comes to forming an opinion of people, after which you won't let your opinion be changed by any lingering doubts. Happily, some six months ago I'd been in a rather similar situation and that was what helped me decide to go back on Mount Everest. I've never regretted it.

Einstein himself said that intuition is the most valuable attribute we have, and was not ashamed to admit that it was this cryptic wisdom which had led him to the Theory of Relativity.

Malcolm Gladwell, the author of *Blink*, describes how in the first two seconds of seeing or experiencing a situation we can know if a tennis player is going to make a good serve, or if a couple will have a future together, or if an art historian is holding a forged vase. He explains how an impression which doesn't seem to be completely rational is much faster and more correct than a conscious decision.

An early warning

The next day, May 9th, while we were at Camp III, our Sherpas were running up and down between Camps II, III and IV. They were taking advantage of this break to get more material up there, when one of the lads, Jangbu, called us on the radio.

One of the members of the Taiwanese expedition, Chen Yu-Nan, had taken a fall when he went to pee without putting on his boots. After sliding for a few meters over the ice, he had fallen into one of the crevasses. Some Sherpas had got him out of there and were helping him climb down, but things weren't looking too good.

As that was going on, a long line of ants was moving along the Lhotse Wall, heading for Camp IV.

Jangbu called us again to tell us that he'd joined the rescue team. Chen Yu-Nan died during the descent. His only colleague on the expedition, Makalu Gau, continued on to Camp IV.

For a Sherpa, the body of a dead person on the mountain is a bad omen. They believe that it brings bad luck, which is why they are reluctant to carry down or even touch a corpse on the mountain.

At all events, Chen had ended up hanging from the fixed ropes half way along the wall, and he couldn't be left there. We went to collect that rigid, inert body, and took it down to the base of the wall, away from the main route.

Everything was covered with a thick, sad fog. First we'd had to beat a retreat, and now we'd been witnesses to this calamity.

Very uncomfortable and ill at ease, I thought that from now on things could only get better. How wrong I was! What we had just been through was only the tip of the iceberg. I couldn't know it, but the worst of all was still to come.

Timeline of the tragedy

What happened over the next few hours was highly confusing, first because of the chaos at Camp IV itself and later because of poor radio communication. Although we were in Camp II, not far from Camp IV, talking over the radio became almost impossible, so Camp IV talked directly with Base Camp, which sent the information to us at Camp II.

Have you ever played the Telephone Game, oi?

On the 10th, some thirty-three people left Camp IV with the aim of reaching the summit of Everest. Some were experienced Himalaya climbers, others were trained mountaineers, but most of the group were amateurs. All in all, there were two commercial expeditions and a third made up of a single Taiwanese member who needed to be guided.

The day went on and we could, from our vantage point below, use binoculars to follow a small stretch of the ascent. The coloured dots were moving too slowly and were an hour behind schedule. The wind was blowing hard; it was not a good day.

Clouds blocked out the summit, and we went back to our tents.

We weren't about to get a full night's sleep. When it was still dark, in the early morning, we were woken up by the radios. There were a lot of people on those expeditions who hadn't come back to the Camp IV tents, and were now caught up in a major storm.

For the time being, all we could do was wait for more news in order to know what was really going on. Even so, it was impossible to put all the different pieces of information together in a way that made sense.

A little before 4.30 pm, Rob Hall started to ask for help for his client, who was close to the summit. Anatoli, one of the guides who had reached the summit without oxygen and had already returned to the camp, had gone out again at around 7 pm with bottles of oxygen to look for other clients who hadn't come back, but had to turn around due to lack of visibility.

Little by little, those who had returned and were up to it, went looking in the tents, some of them now badly ripped, to see who was missing. Some twenty people were unaccounted for, eleven of whom were at 300 meters distance from the tents, lost in the middle of the South Col, curled up without light or oxygen, holding out against the cold and the wind.

Around midnight, after five hours spent waiting for their deaths, a brief patch of blue made it possible for them to intuitively work out where the camp was. The six who could still walk took almost an hour to find and reach Camp IV.

At this camp there were two different groups of tired, exhausted climbers. Both were trying to do something about the situation, but between them they didn't know what, they couldn't communicate.

Out of all of them, the only one with enough energy to finally come out of there was Anatoli, who went off to look for the five who were lost on the terrace. The other climbers were worn out and the Sherpas who hadn't been exhausted by the climb had been poisoned by the carbon monoxide from the camping stoves.

When Anatoli found this group of five, just a few meters from the precipice on the other side of the mountain, he could only take them back one by one. First he took Charlotte, and when he got back, Yakuso was already dead and Beck had disappeared, so he took Sandy, while Madsen dragged himself along without help.

They reached the camp in the early daylight, around five in the morning. More or less at the same time, Rob was still at the South Summit, at 8,750 meters. He was alive, but with frostbite that made it impossible for him to come back down and he was too tired to try, anyhow. His client, Doug, was dead.

The journalist Jon Krakauer, who wrote *Into Thin Air*, was also exhausted by the altitude and by the climb to the summit the day before. He went on trying to fit different snippets of information together and communicated with us by radio until the battery ran out.

Our frustration became even harder to cope with when Woodall - who formed part of the South African expedition, which hadn't made it to the summit - was asked to please give Jon a radio, he refused.

The fifty oxygen bottles which we had stored at Camp IV for our ascent to the summit, along with batteries, camping gas and food, were placed at the disposition of whoever needed them.

Meanwhile, there were still people who hadn't come back and who couldn't even be located: the Taiwanese Makalu Gau and two guides, Scott and Andy. Doug, Yakuso and Beck were already dead, and a few of those who were at the camp would die soon if we couldn't manage to get them out of there fast. Some were unconscious, and others, delirious.

The day after

The following morning, the 11th, Camp IV was still receiving chaotically relayed, half-digested information. Although there was some visibility, the storm was still raging, more so, even, than the previous day. The wind was blowing so strongly, it sounded like a jet engine had been pressed to our ears.

At 9.30 am two Sherpas went to look for Rob. At 3 pm, some 200 meters from where he was, the wind forced them to turn back. Nobody would be going to look for Rob that afternoon. The last time we heard his voice, was during the farewell conversation he had with his wife, who was in New Zealand.

That same day, in the morning, a mountaineer who happened to be a doctor found the energy, along with the help of two Sherpas, to go out and look for the bodies of Yakuso and Beck. He found them half buried in the snow, without their gloves on, comatose and unconscious, but, surprisingly, they were still breathing.

He came back to the camp to gather together the people who weren't unconscious or delirious to see what could be done, but nobody had enough energy to bring the two who were outside into the tents. Had they done so, the two would probably have died anyway after a short while and it was impossible to send them further down the mountain in that storm.

One of the guides started to head down with a small group of clients, who were connected to their oxygen and had been injected with dexamethasone, a powerful anti-inflammatory drug which works well when it comes to helping people recover briefly at high altitude, but only if they're going downhill.

We went on climbing and intercepted them at Camp III, where for the time being we set things up so we could provide them with hot drinks. We didn't let them stay, as they had to go down to Camp II, at the very least.

I was discouraged, surprised and even angered by the behaviour of some of those people. Charlotte, in a loud voice, as if she were at a party, went about telling everybody she'd reached the summit. She talked and smiled, happy for herself, when all around her there were people who had died and many who were struggling to save those who were still alive, handing over their materials and resources, risking their lives and abandoning their own projects.

I too should have injected myself with something because after that meeting, I felt nothing. No fear, no pain, no sadness. Nothing.

The miracle ofn Beck Waters

All of a sudden, half-way through the afternoon, another person appeared at Camp IV. They saw him walking towards them from a distance, looking like a scarecrow, fighting against the wind that was blowing into his face.

It wasn Beck. Nobody could believe it, as they'd given him up for dead.

He was blind in one eye and could only see with difficulty through the other one, and he was staggering from side to side.

They put him in an empty, slightly damaged tent. They laid him down and put some sleeping bags over him. But nobody attended to him during the night, because it was impossible for him survive another day in those conditions. It has taken much less to kill people in similar situations. It is unthinkable that anyone could survive who has been subjected to so many hours of cold – up to 50° below zero[2]. Up there, it takes very little for you to start to give in, to let yourself go and for your body to stop fighting.

The three Sherpas who had gone to look for Scott and Makalu Gau found them at three hundred meters above the camp. Scott was half unconscious and it was impossible to move him, so they left him there. Makalu Gau, although badly injured and frozen, came down after he'd had ropes attached to him, but he was walking under his own steam.

Seeing that they were coming back without Scott, Anatoli didn't resign himself to the situation and went up to look for him, but found him dead in an unusual position. He'd half-way undressed himself. It would seem that in the final moments of a cerebral oedema or a hypothermia, mountaineers feel warm and try to remove their clothes.

After that terrible discovery, Anatoli came back down late at night, caught in a second storm in which he was almost lost.

---

[2] If we add in the wind factor, the apparent temperature is lower. At -50°C with a 40km/h wind, the apparent temperature is -90°C. At 0°C, a 40km/h wind will give an apparent temperature of -15C.

On the 12th, everybody went back down. There was nobody else left to wait for. When they were about to leave the camp, they heard cries coming from one of the tents.

Against all the odds, Beck was still alive and was in a very bad mood. His tent was open, the wind had ripped the sleeping bags off him and he'd been shouting for two hours.

We heard the news in Camp III but we didn't think anything could be done for him. Beck was also given some dexamethasone and a short while later he stood up.

Robert and Ed started to climb half-way up to join those who were helping him down. When he reached Camp III and I finally saw him, I couldn't believe it. The man was a complete wreck! His cheeks were black and frozen, his beard was full of frozen, bloody mucus, his hands were stiff, frozen and black all the way up to the elbows.
He must have gone two days without food...and I didn't want to ask him, but I imagine he must have wet himself.

In his place, I would have wanted to die and stop suffering, but he, on the contrary, made a joke of it all. He had fought against all the elements, against all the catastrophic predictions; he had proven all the survival probability charts wrong. He'd saved himself through sheer willpower, with a conscious decision not to let himself be overcome, from the moment he'd woken up in the middle of the South Col.

We spent the whole afternoon getting him down. We went faster than we'd expected and by the end of the afternoon we reached the base of the Wall: Camp II.

Once there, there was no need to fear for his death or for that of Makalu Gau. There were doctors and medicines ready to help them recover. Their frostbite was another matter, as that couldn't be treated until they reached a hospital.

We breathed a sigh of relief. We'd overcome yet one more obstacle, but the following day came the most complicated part: crossing the icefall from Camp I to Base Camp.

We went to sleep and I continued to feel I'd been internally anaesthetised. I reacted quickly, I did my work and took the initiative, but was bereft of feelings. It was as if everything was happening behind a barrier of transparent jelly which wouldn't allow my emotions to be affected. I thought about that night, when I went to bed: "What's happening to me? Am I such a bad person that I don't feel any kind of sadness?"

It was asking myself those questions that I fell asleep.

A second miracle

The idea of dragging Beck and Makalu Gau down the icefall was not practicable. The whole place was a labyrinth that went uphill and downhill, with flanking walls, sections of metal ladders joined together three at a time in order to cross wide crevasses.

You can only be in this place a few hours and you have to move fast before a block of ice falls or a platform collapses. To attempt an evacuation would be to risk the lives of a lot of people. We would do it if there were no alternative, but we had another other possibility.

Very early the following morning I found out that a pilot from the Nepalese army would try and reach us by helicopter so as to pick up Beck and Makalu Gau half-way between Camps I and II.

They took quite a while to find the best place for the helicopter to land, not that we were that sure they would. Until then there hadn't been many attempts to do this kind of thing, and the pilots who had tried it had ended up crashing.

In a nutshell, at this altitude the air is so rarefied that the helicopter blades don't have anything to give them lift. The motor also doesn't function works as well as usual, because it has less oxygen for its combustion. So the motor needs to be modified so it can move the blades with greater force, and the helicopter has to weigh very little. That's not something you can get ready in a day.

David found a good flat area, free of crevasses, but we had to mark it out so the helicopter could see it.

Suddenly, we heard a noise. We couldn't believe it! A pilot had decided to attempt this all but suicidal mission. We had to hurry and mark out the right spot. David started to yell that he needed a handkerchief on a stick, something to serve as a marker for the landing area.

I threw him my water bottle with berry-flavoured Kool-Aid, my favourite. He looked at me very seriously and said:

"I'm not thirsty right now."

"It's not for that! It's so you can make a big red X on the white snow."

He smiled, surprised, and started to run.

The helicopter didn't make one but two trips, one for Makalu Gau, who couldn't walk and got out first, and the other one for Beck, who, for a moment, had thought he'd never get out of that place. This was the highest altitude helicopter rescue in history.

HAVING THE COURAGE TO TRY

Colonel Madan Khatri Chhetri, the pilot of the Royal Nepalese Armed Forces who had dared to fly that mission, was a very special person. Aside from his skill as a pilot, he knew what needed to be done and had emptied the helicopter of everything that wasn't needed, including some fuel.

Many successes in life are the result of our having got rid of something that seemed necessary.

He was lucky to have such calm weather that day, but colonel Madanm Khatri Chhetri had something that's difficult to find: he was ready to try, and his superiors didn't tell him it couldn't be done before he did so.

The simple fact of trying something, no matter how daring it might seem, makes it more likely that we'll succeed in doing it. To try and do something when there's an obstacle or a situation that needs dealing with, is like putting your foot in a door that's about to shut.

Many milestones, discoveries and advances in the history of humanity have been achieved because one single person was prepared to try.

The ghost camp

We went on climbing downhill. I think I was with Jamling, who was often at my side. I remember hardly anything of the journey to Base Camp that day, merely a certain peculiar feeling when we passed the chaotic Khumbu icefall.

On the way up, I'd thought with some jubilation "this'll be the last time I do this. When I come here on my way down, it'll be because I'm on my way back home." But I wasn't on my way down because I'd reached the summit. I was passing by without knowing if we were going to try for the summit again. In fact, at that precise moment, I didn't know anything. The anaesthesia would still take a few days to wear off.

When you get back from a higher camp, the people at Base Camp always greet you with enthusiasm. You all sit down at the table and chat, and have something to drink. This time, however, the welcome was silent, full of questioning looks, with averted eyes by way of a response.

There were plenty of phone calls from the American press, who wanted to know what had happened. Fortunately for me, the news didn't have much impact at home, although this kind of disaster is a staple for the mountaineering sections of most media. At all events, the communication networks of the time, lacking emails and websites, meant that I could stay fairly calm during this period.

We needed a few days to rest, recover and decide what we wanted to do.

Base Camp emptied the day after the funeral: a small ceremony for the six people who had died during those three days. What a frost-like feeling there was, and everything was so grey... How could everything have changed so much in such a short time?

It was no longer a pleasant colourful camp, but a soulless place. Walking among the now empty tents felt like walking through a ghost town. There, where a few days ago you could hear music and the cooks singing, and there were people strolling up and down, all that was left were the remains of what had once been the kitchens. The walls of stones that had been fireplaces, blackened by the fumes from kerosene lamps, were about to collapse.

Where there had once been tents, all that was left was a stone platform, which had risen into the air once the surrounding ice had melted, forming towers without any princesses in them. The remains of prayer banners were piled up, damp, on the ground. The left-overs that some porter hadn't wanted to clear away due to lethargy or haste, made the scene look even sadder.

Was it cold or was I just feeling nervous?

I spent two days turning all this over in my mind. Little by little, the pieces began to fall into place. The members of our team were still getting along well together, that's for sure, and our camp was my island. When I got back, I was safe. We tried to make jokes, not to make each other laugh but to remind each other that we were there to do whatever was necessary.

I still had to find out what I wanted to do. As I was in a state of confusion, I started by asking myself what I *didn't* want to do.

MOTIVATION GONE ASTRAY

Do you want to leave it be? Do you want to go back home? From the bottom of my heart, the very idea of doing that was painful to me. No, I didn't want to leave it be. I didn't want to abandon a project in which I believed and in which I'd invested so much effort. I didn't want to abandon a group which together had achieved so many things and of which I was proud to form a part.

If I went home the next day, I knew what would happen: nothing. If I stayed, I would once again find myself surrounded by uncertainties, and that is what attracted me.

Monotony and certainty bore me. To feel alive, I've learnt to enjoy not knowing that's going to happen next. If I was afraid, it was of leaving without even having made an attempt to go ahead; something I would never have forgiven myself for. It wasn't a question of reaching the summit, or not anymore; to an extent, that was the least important thing. The main thing was to dare to face the challenge.

Ed said something at the time that made a lot of sense: we couldn't go away leaving behind the idea that Everest is a place where people die. On the contrary, we had to climb up, reach the summit, and make it clear that things can be done properly.

If you've ever had a clear, thought-out motive for doing something, it's possible that your motivation could go astray. I say "astray" because I don't believe that you can actually lose your motivation. If you really want to do something, you have to have a reason for doing it. If you don't have a reason, you don't have a motive, and there is therefore no real motivation.

Sometimes we don't lose our motivation, it's just that we never had it in the first place. We do something because someone has said that we have to do it, because it's good for us, or because it's a tradition, but that doesn't convince us. We haven't made that decision from the bottom of our hearts, we don't have a motive.

We let our motivation go astray at times and in situations when we feel overcome by circumstances. But if you have a reason, that will be strong enough to get you back on your feet again. You'll find it hard to weaken or to leave things be.

Even Jack the Ripper had motivation; whether his goal was a correct one or not is another matter.

Another chance

On the morning of the 16th, each of us, separately, without any kind of outside pressure being brought to bear, and knowing we had the freedom to leave whenever we wanted to, came to the same conclusion: we had to give the mountain another chance.

That decided, we began to organise ourselves for the ascent.

There were two main obstacles that we had to overcome: the material which had been used up on Camp IV during the rescue: we needed to re-equip that camp, at least.

The Sherpas would play the most decisive role in all of this. They'd already done their work, they'd accomplished everything they were supposed to do and for which they were being paid.

Something which Jon Krakauer wrote in his book and which later was played up, thus distorting the truth, was that our expedition cost five and half million dollars, and that that was motivation enough for us to continue after the tragedy.

It's possible that this was the price the production house spent, bearing in mind that each roll of film cost more or less two thousand dollars, the astronomical price of the camera, and the cost of all the post-production, including music by George Harrison and the narrative voice-over by Liam Neeson...who said my name during his presentation, which was quite simply priceless.

I imagine that Jon confused the cost of the expedition with what we were earning, but these were clearly two very different things.

I in particular had a salary of 9,000€ for a total of three months' work. Money which at that time I badly needed; a sum, however, which didn't warrant me risking my life.

By contrast, it was deeply moving to see how the porters had no intention of going back home. They felt as much a part of this project as we did. If they became so seriously involved, in such a short time and at all levels, it meant that we were doing something right.

So we had a team, but we needed to get hold of the equipment that was lacking: above all, ropes, gas and oxygen, because after the rescue, the supplies which we'd stored in Camp IV had all but disappeared.

We went around scavenging what we could from the other expeditions as we prepared to leave. We were working against the clock, given that in less than two days everyone else would have gone. Finally, we decided that if we rationed our intake and took the minimum amount possible, we still had a chance. All we needed was for the weather to hold.

Starting over

We already knew the route and climbed very quickly up to Camp II, well acclimatised and without stopping to film. The camera had remained at Camp III.

When I was crossing one of the crevasses, balancing on the metal ladder and holding the ropes with both hands, fitting the crampons into the metal bars, the ladder began to sway as it caught up by a wave. Then I thought: "right, now every step I take is going to get me to the end of this; don't think about the difficulty or how tired you are, take advantage of the moment, enjoy it, because you're never going to experience such a moment again".

The road map had to be corrected once more, when we saw that the weather wasn't looking good. We needed to be pinpoint accurate. We weren't carrying any extra material, and nobody would come to help us if we ran into any problems. We were alone, just as we'd always wanted, so we could film in peace, although of course we'd never wanted to be in this situation because of a recent catastrophe.

On the way to Camp IV we started to move over terrain that was new for us, full of history though it was.

We stopped to film, so as to keep our hand in.

When you reach Camp IV, the last delicate stretch involves getting over a place known as the Geneva Spur. Its history contains many valuable lessons which I have never forgotten since I first read about it.

In 1952, a year before the father of my colleague on the ropes and Hillary reached the summit, a group of Swiss made the first expedition across the valley. They were the first to deal with this completely unknown territory, without knowing where it was possible to climb, where there were avalanches, and yet they found the key to the two main stretches along this route: the Khumbu icefall and the Genever Spur at 7,986 meters.

Nobody now remembers the names of those people: Raymond Lambert, René Aubert and Leon Flory, together with Tensing Norgay, who would come back the following year and manage, for the first time in history, to climb up to the South Summit at 8,760 meters.

In 1953, a couple of days before Hillary and Tensing (who had been hired because the year before he'd been with the expedition that that had resolved the cruxes of the matter[3]), reached the summit, Bourdillon and Evans set foot on the South Summit, but a problem with their oxygen masks made them turn back. The information that they passed on to Hillary and Tenzing, however, proved essential for these two to reach the summit.

Who achieves the objective first is the one who gets all the honours. Those who open up the route, if they come in second, remain completely unknown. We should take care of our heroes and be a little more curious and sceptical about history. We should never lose sight of the fact that a major success is not the result of an isolated feat, but rather is the outcome of many earlier sacrifices, trials and errors. Fortune often behaves in a fickle manner and history is often unfair, denying as it does recognition to those who made so many things possible.

It was with these thoughts that I stood on the black ridge of the Spur and looked at the summit of Everest. Before me, I had the final pyramid of granite and ice, imposing, noble and majestic.

I would have to wait until the following day, to see what was going to happen during the final assault.

EVERYTHING STARTS WITH A THOUGHT

Base Camp had been abandoned for ten days, nobody had set foot in it for ten days. And there we were, yet again, with our crampons, pricking the mountainside, disturbing its peace and quiet.

I tried to tread softly, calmly, with respect, so as not to disturb the mountain, so it would accept me, so it would let me climb it.

---

[3] When climbing, the most difficult part of a route isn't always the one which is technically more difficult, but rather the difficulty lies in finding the access point which allows you to continue the ascent.

The Inuit believe that everything on Earth has a spirit: animals and the elements, a valley, a tree, a river, a rock, the wind, a mountain. When we don't respect nature or the elements, then we offend the spirits, which show their displeasure with droughts, earthquakes or storms.

The mountain didn't speak to me, but I spoke to it. I believe in showing respect to everything around us, people, animals, and nature, and talking to the mountain with my thoughts, was my way of respecting it. For Buddhists, our thoughts and actions determine who we are and each moment of life offers us an infinite series of possibilities: to change, to improve, or to spoil everything. I didn't look at that pyramid in fear, but rather with respect; not with ambition, but with humility.

III. Who Invented Failure?

Some defeats are more triumphant than victories.

MICHEL DE MONTAIGNE

When I heard the horn of the forklift truck, I ran out as fast as I could. This was the signal. I got up from the wooden case where I was sitting in a shadowy corner, I put down the book I was reading and went to open one of the five doors of the cold storage room.

The corridor was long and wide, with a cold, dark cement floor. Signalling from afar, Joan indicated which was the right door and I ran as fast as I could. I ran in order to tire myself out – just sitting there was a bore – and because I wanted to do the work as best I could so they wouldn't replace me with someone else.

It was a bore, yes, but it was better than spending ten or twelve hours a day during the endless, hot summer canning fruit, in silence, on a production line. I never understood why they didn't let us talk there. I was sixteen.

One day they picked me out, perhaps because the fork lift driver had asked them to, who knows? At all events, they assigned me to opening and closing doors so that the loads of fruit could come in or go out. I sat in a corner of the corridor, which I would sweep and then I'd sit back down to twiddle my thumbs. Until one day, when the boss walked past, I asked him if I could read while I was sitting.

The last few meters before reaching the summit aren't difficult for me. Once I'm up there, I sit down and let my feet dangle over the abyss.

"What are you reading?" the boss asked me.

"Reinhold Messner, *The Crystal Horizon: Everest – The First Solo Ascent.*"

And I gave him a big smile of satisfaction.

He looked at me in an odd way.

At sixteen, I didn't know what I wanted to be or what I wanted to do, but I was very sure of one thing: I didn't want to bore myself to death in a job. I didn't want to have to look at my watch every ten minutes as I did when I was canning peaches, seeing that time wasn't moving forward and that one hour seemed like an eternity. Just thinking about monotony made me fall into a dark hole in which my soul felt as if it were suffocating.

I also didn't know that maybe one day I'd go to Everest.

There are people who knew they would do so even when they were little; I've met some. I didn't, but at the time, I liked that book very much. Who knows if it left some kind of imprint on my subconscious.

The North Face of Everest

"Twenty-three kilos? That's not possible, yours weighs twenty-two..."

I couldn't understand how he'd done it. My rucksack weighed a kilo more than Néstor's, and we'd shared everything out in equal amounts, as fairly as possible. Ernest's weighed even more, so I kept my mouth shut.

We left our lonely camp so as to acclimatise ourselves, away from the route we'd chosen. This is how things are done according to the authentic alpine style: you acclimatise yourself as best you can, and when you're ready, you follow your route without fixed ropes, without porters, without ready-pitched camps and without oxygen.

The route along what is known as the Hornbein Couloir, on Everest's North Face, was waiting for us. 2,500 meters of a neat, direct line straight to the summit, by means of a wall which presented technical difficulties and which was vertical in those places where it turned into a gorge. But beforehand, we had to acclimatise ourselves well.

It was the autumn of 1995 and I was twenty-five years old.

Walking more than 5000 meters with 23 kilos on your back is a torture I would not recommend to anybody...not anywhere, not even at sea level. It took us two days to go from our Base Camp, located at the end of the Rongbuk Glacier, to the Base Camp on the normal Everest route via the North Face.

We were carrying food for three days and it took us seven. We were also carrying a tent for Base Camp, in which we all had to fit. It was a tent designed for two people to be comfortable in, or even three; maybe four people could, in an emergency, fit in uncomfortably. There were six of us.

We slept head to toe and on our sides. It was impossible to stretch out fully: when one person wanted to turn, we all had to. We breakfasted there and we had supper there. There was no lunch, we didn't have enough food. One midday, we found Gigi had lit the camping stove and was heating up some water:

"Gigi, what are you doing? We don't have any food...

"Well, just in case!"

I think he was just kidding himself, like we all were, but he was going about it in a somewhat peculiar way.

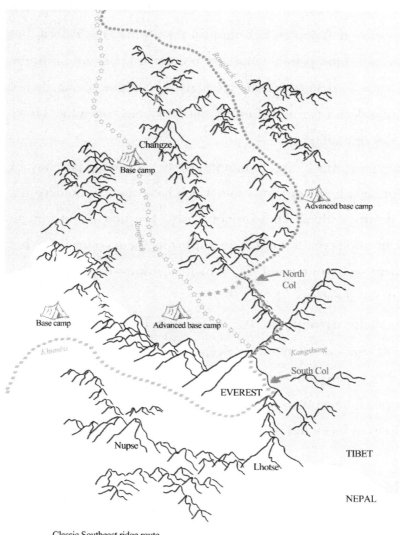

Changze

Base camp

Advanced base camp

Rongbuck Esote

Rongbuck

North
Col

Base camp

Advanced base camp

Khumbu

Kangshung

South Col

EVEREST

Nupse

Lhotse

TIBET

NEPAL

- – – – Classic Southeast ridge route
- •••••• Classic North ridge route
- ☆ ☆ ☆ ☆ Japonese route + Hornbein Couloir
- ✻ ✻ ✻ ✻ Access varaint to the North

MIND GAMES

Everybody uses mind games to sidestep a painful, uncomfortable, dull or tough situation. You can face up to it for a while, live with it, but when it becomes too painful you have to cover it up, or lose it in the maze of your own imagination. It's a matter of not seeing it, not hearing it, and you can transform it into anything you want. How? Using games or meditation.

There are jobs which are monotonous, like canning peaches or walking for eight hours on a moraine which has countless bothersome ups and downs, with 23 kilos on your back. I've now learnt how to deal with situations of this kind. You mustn't let them control you, but master them with your mind. It's a matter of knowing how to play games with the situation.

Meditation helps us to prevent the anxiety that comes from monotony by concentrating our attention on deep, conscious breathing, but any other way we can find to occupy our thoughts – for example, remembering a long poem or memorising words in a foreign language – can help us to focus and put an end to our worries.

A matter of proportion

After spending two nights on the North Col, at 7,000 meters, we returned to our Base Camp more or less acclimatised and a lot thinner.

Since then we spent all our time making trips with loads of material and food, as well as setting up the tents of what will be our advance Base Camp, just at the foot of the Hornbein Couloir. It was a vast plateau of snow which, because the mountain itself is also huge, looked as if it were in proportion to it.

We weren't able to realise just how large it really was until we contrasted it with something we knew the real size of. We were unable to take in or fully understand the dimensions involved.

We quickly got a clear idea on the day we entered the glacier and marked out a particular rock as our next destination. We worked out we'd get there in fifteen minutes. In the end it took us over two hours and the rock turned out to be the size of the Sphinx...If all the proportions were like this, we could not afford to underestimate the wall we had before us. Logically enough, it had much larger dimensions and longer distances than our eyes could perceive at first sight.

For the same reason, if it snowed it would be impossible to find the tents. We had to mark them with very tall poles, so that they wouldn't get lost in all that immensity.

The risks of not knowing English

At Base Camp we had communication via satellite, although that kind of technology was still in its early days as far as using it on mountains was concerned. The device and the aerial fitted into a box the size of an attaché case and we had to find the position of the satellite each time we wished to establish a connection, something which wasn't always possible.

It was my first experience of this technology on an expedition, as it was for Gigi, who nearly ruined everything in ten seconds flat. We were playing cards in the dining tent when he stuck his head through the zip entrance and asked:

"What does 'delete' mean?"

Holding up his cards and without looking at him, Albert answered, in Catalan:

"*Esborrar.*"

"And 'delete all'?"

Nobody said anything, but we looked at each other with wide open eyes and raised eyebrows. The cards were tossed up into the air, the chairs were knocked over and Ernest and Albert rushed out, bumping into the doorway, to get to the communications tent as fast as possible, where we'd left the box with the satellite phone and the computer, the screen of which had gone blank with a blinking white cursor on it.

Just as well those two were engineering students: they slowly managed to recover the missing information, which was to be found, fragmented and in disorder, in the hard drive. Even so, not everything was saved. We had to do the best we could in order to go on communicating and receiving the weather reports, which weren't that accurate in any case.

From that day on, we gave Gigi a pencil and paper and an English dictionary.

We found ourselves quite alone on that route. At Base Camp there was only one other expedition made up of two New Zealanders who were taking a nearby route: the Norton Couloir. They, too, wanted to do it in the alpine style. They were just as crazy as we were.

THE ROAD NOT TAKEN

This is a solitary, empty Base Camp. Nobody ever comes here. Many of the expeditions that want to climb Everest choose the two usual routes: either the Nepalese slope that takes you up the South Face, or the Tibetan slope which takes you up via the North Ridge. But nobody usually climbs where we were, where the routes are more difficult, technically complex and potentially risky. Which means that there are few possibilities of reaching the summit, but at the same time, from my point of view, it's a neater, more attractive challenge, with less crowds.

Our choice has always made me think about the way in which we choose what to do. What are we looking for when we set a goal for ourselves? To achieve it no matter what and at any cost? With quantity outdoing quality? What is it that we find satisfying: that everybody should appreciate what we do, as if it were something incredible? Or that a small number of more specialised people can value what we've done or are trying to do? Are we climbing for ourselves or for other people? What do we want? To get things right, to use all means possible, just in order to accumulate a pile of achieved goals? Or are we trying to look for something unique, even though that almost certainly means that we'll have to make a greater effort and achieve less? This is a decision that needs to be taken into account not only by who's selling but also by who's buying.

A famous poem by Robert Frost, *The Road Not Taken*, talks about a traveller who has to make precisely this decision and ends thus:

Two roads diverged in a wood, and I –
I took the one less travelled by,
And that has made all the difference.

A difficult route

The New Zealanders left without reaching the summit and after being hit by an avalanche. Immediately afterwards, an American passed by our Base Camp before heading home, also thanks to an avalanche on his route, and days later he would make a hasty proposal to me about a documentary, which I rejected.

After all this, the time came for us to start the climb up, and to be honest I was feeling nervous. Ahead of us was one of the most demanding routes in the Himalayas, not only because of the technical difficulties, but also because the steepness of the route made it impossible to set up any camps. So we were obliged to reach a certain point before we could sleep. There was no stopping until then.

There had to be a good reason why, up until then, only nine people in the whole world had managed to reach the summit via this route.

At first sight, the way in which we wanted to scale this mountain might seem ill-advised, but it was anything but. Our choice was a result of our convictions about how we wanted to do things and of a decision that had been thought out to the last detail. To move lightly and fast while not having to acclimatise ourselves *in situ* minimised the dangers. The less time we were up there, and the faster we moved on, the less chances there were that we'd be swept away by an avalanche or that we'd suffer an oedema from the altitude.

On the other hand, it was going to be tougher than an ascent via a normal route or using the classical style, as we didn't have any fixed ropes to grasp hold of, nor an open trail, nor pre-prepared tents. But when we'd weighed up the pros and cons, we reckoned the alpine style was what was best.

The time of the ascent

It was autumn, the post-monsoon season, and it was colder than in the pre-monsoon season, which is in spring. We left in the early morning, around one or two, totally concentrated and silent, one after the other.

We headed over to the wall, Ernest, Manel, Ferran, Gigi and I, as our crampons bit into the hard snow, making a short, muffled, dry sound.

We scaled the wall without a word; the slope was very steep: about 45º. We couldn't make any mistakes, because we weren't fastened to any ropes; neither were we carrying ropes and each person had to look out for him or herself. If somebody were to decide to give up, it couldn't be allowed to affect the rest of us. That person had to be technically prepared, strong and sure enough of himself to be able to go back down alone. In other words, **you can't give up when you're at the end of your tether so that someone has to help you back down because you're unable to make it on your own.** You have to give up when you feel tired. **To go on until you've reached your limit means that someone will have to risk their life helping you to go back down, relinquishing his or her dream.** You have to learn to know yourself so that you can leave a safe margin for any retreat and, above all, you can't be so selfish as to assume that someone will risk their life to help you, among other things because they sometimes don't.

We were moving slowly, but at a good, steady pace. We were more than 6,000 meters above sea level. I was concentrating hard, but felt reasonably optimistic. We spent the entire night climbing, and the snow was starting to get obstinate. The sound it made when we trod on it sounded hollower and hollower, and around us, everything seemed to be crumbling.

After a long while waiting to see if conditions were going to change, given that it was just a matter of a short stretch, we realised how things were turning out and ended up calculating that the situation was highly dangerous. We were moving over a sheet of windswept snow which could break up and make us fall back down. We were at a height of nearly 7,000 meters: so we decided to beat a retreat.

The descent was more complicated than the ascent; we were climbing down with our backs to the wall, taking care not to make any false steps, which would have sent us into a fall all the way down the thousand meters we'd just ascended.

We went straight to the tents, without exchanging a word. Nobody regretted the decision, but it was difficult to accept that in a few seconds we'd abandoned our dream after working on it for two years.

The last chance

When we woke up at midday, I think it was Ernst who suggested something really crazy: our last option. It was a brilliant, spontaneous idea. To go from where we were to the North Ridge and go up from there to the summit, taking advantage of a section of the normal route. That is to say: we would enter the normal Tibetan route from behind, starting from our advanced Base Camp and going to their Base Camp, and at a height of 7,000 meters, we would head for the North Col.

What's more, this was something that had never been done before. All we needed was luck with the weather over that stretch: we had enough material and food. That's the advantage of the alpine style: you're self-sufficient and can improvise as long as you've got provisions. You carry everything on your back, like a snail.

We quickly got very enthusiastic: we still had a final option, a chance. We weren't about to leave without exhausting all the possibilities.

We left the next day, early in the morning. Due to the direction the wall was facing, there were less possibilities that we'd find windswept sheets, but nonetheless were fully alert and focussed as we climbed.

It was steep slope and once again we were moving without ropes, but that wasn't the greatest difficulty, the real problem was that we didn't have any information. We were improvising and none of us had done that before, at least as far as we knew. Which is why we didn't have any exact indications about this stretch, something which, in emotional terms, can be very exhausting. When you know what you're dealing with, you can prepare yourself. When you don't, you have to be a lot more vigilant.

There was almost a thousand meters of unknown, irregular terrain. When you're moving along a path where there's nobody else and where maybe nobody else has ever been before, your fears are different from the kind you feel when taking a beaten path.

The toughest decision

We reached the North Col at midday. It was extremely cold, but we were on the North Ridge, the usual Everest route. There was another expedition, that was over a day ahead of us.

After resting for the night, the next day it was so cold I couldn't even put my crampons on. It was sheer hell to fold the tent so we could move on in the small hours. A steady, icy wind was blowing.

By the time it was daylight, it had been a while since I'd been unable to get my toes back to their normal temperature. That wasn't serious at that particular moment, but if I didn't do something about it, it would have ended up being so, so I told my colleagues that I was going to turn back.

I felt strong, and was keeping up the pace despite a heavy rucksack, but if I couldn't get down that mountain without all my fingers, that didn't mean a thing.

WITH A LITTLE HELP FROM MY FRIENDS

We all have priorities. For me a mountain summit isn't one of them and what's more I don't want to risk the lives of my colleagues who would have to help me down, just because of my selfishness in wanting to achieve a personal goal. But Ernest and Ferran stopped and decided to warm up my feet using their bodies, in the hope that by the time the sun rose my normal temperature would have returned. And also because we were a team. Sometimes a small personal sacrifice, such as stopping and slowing up the pace, can contribute something to a group which would be weaker were it to lose one of its members. We spent almost an hour working on my feet and when I'd recovered, my feet warm again, we went on climbing up to Camp II at 7,900 meters.

The refrain from the Beatles' song goes: **"I get by with a little help from my friends"** and that's an important lesson whether on a mountain or in life generally. As important as good preparation and trust is **allowing yourself to be helped at those moments when you seem to have run into an insuperable obstacle, for whatever reason.** Things which seemed impossible on an individual basis, can become surprisingly feasible with a little help from those around us, who, being more objective, can see other solutions to the problem.

That afternoon I called Base Camp on the radio. I'd decided that the following day, while the others went on climbing, I would withdraw for good. The wind was blowing steadily and it was getting colder and colder. It was obvious that as we went on climbing, it would get even colder. The lack of oxygen was an additional difficulty, given that it meant I was more likely to freeze.

I made the decision, then cancelled it and confirmed it several more times. My willpower urged me to go on climbing, but my better judgement told me to go back down. I was strong, well-trained, and motivated by a fantastic team, but I felt I had to make the descent. If you don't take account of just one small detail you can ruin your life and maybe that of others.

It was the first time I'd taken such a serious decision, and that, too, made me doubtful. Years later, experience would tell me that it's not a mistake to withdraw in time, but is rather an opportunity to do things better the next time around.

An example of willpower and mastery over one's limits

I went down 1,500 meters in one go. Gigi followed, because he didn't feel so good and also wanted to go back down. Ernest, Ferran and Manel went on climbing.

Albert, who had decided days ago that he wanted to quit and had stayed behind as back-up at Base Camp, had come to look for us from the other side of the mountain so as to bring us food and some footwear that was more comfortable than the boots we were wearing. Otherwise, we would have had to do the 17 kilometers which separated the two base camps with heavy high altitude boots.

The next day, Ernest, Ferran and Manel withdrew at 8,500 meters because of the cold. Manel had frostbite on his nose.

I felt a growing admiration for Ernest. He had been diagnosed as a Class I diabetic just a year and a half ago: he was dependent on insulin.

I remember the afternoon before they took him to the hospital. We'd been at his place, making meringues. I've always thought that that had something to do with it. The only time I ever saw him downhearted was when the doctors in the hospital told him that he could never go mountaineering again. He was twenty-seven.

A few days afterwards, he got hold of a load of books in order to understand what it was he had. After buying all the different types of insulin, with their different rates of absorption, along with glucose meters, glycogen and other things, he put the lot on the table. He explored where the obstacles lay and which tools were at hand to overcome them. He knew exactly what he wanted and never lost his optimism or the drive which was so typical of him.

A month and a half later we went off to climb the local Pedraforca mountain. That was the first test. A few adjustments had to be made, because from time to time he took too great a dose of insulin and had to eat quickly so as not to faint. In the summer of that year, the Alps served as a testing ground to see how he could handle cold, gloves and several days in the mountains.

Fourteen months later he went off to Everest, stronger than ever.

On Everest he turned back around because there was an icy wind and the conditions were unfit for humans, not because he was diabetic, but as far as I was concerned, that day he reached the summit.

Even today he is the person with diabetes who has climbed highest without oxygen. This is without a doubt, proof of how **willpower, positive attitude, intelligence and passion together can ensure that nothing is impossible, even if some people have told you it is before you've even started.**

A SUCCESSFUL FAILURE

We didn't reach the summit, but I don't feel that we failed in any way. I don't know how or why the concept of failure - which I consider to be an artificial one - is used so often. I came back from this expedition having learnt a very great deal. I gained experience and had discovered new sensations. I took decisions which would prove to be of use for the rest of my life, aside from coming back with all my fingers and toes free from frostbite, and without having risked any of my colleagues' lives. So I went home with my pockets full, so to speak.

To fail would have been to stay there with our arms folded, not doing anything, giving up without trying the last possible option and going home disappointed after all our efforts. We exhausted all the possibilities, we tried everything, we adapted to the changes we came across, and we never felt that we'd given up in any way. All of this made me feel satisfied, rather than feeling like a failure. We had the arrogance of youth, we were without fear and without experience, which is what often motivates enterprising people to **achieve goals, make dreams come true and not to resign themselves.**

One of the feats of the space race was a failure, precisely. The Apollo XIII craft, whose aim was to reach the moon, had to deal with a highly serious technical problem which seemed impossible to solve, thus condemning the crew members to a certain death. From that moment on, the objective changed completely and became that of getting the astronauts safely back to Earth. After an effort of imagination on the part of ground control and the skill and improvisation of the astronauts, they managed to do just that, against all the odds. The expedition was thus considered a "successful failure".

IV. Breaking Paradigms.

If a man wishes to be sure of the road he treads on,

he must close his eyes and walk in the dark.

JUAN DE LA CRUZ

I found it difficult to breathe without grimacing. The streets stank of burnt meat, a bitter, sour smell, but above all it took me an effort to look at the pile of wood.

There was one which was bigger than the others. It must have been a rich man, although he looked thin under the fine linen cloth that covered him. There were more piles, together with covered bodies, near that brownish, dirty river, but none of them was as big as that one. Some of them had been burning for some time, and at others there was just the watchman who stirred the fire so that it eventually turned into ash and would end up in the water.

The sadness in the atmosphere, or at least so I perceived it, was contrasted by and mixed up with the cries of children as they jumped into the water, playing just meters away. Some men had shaved their heads as a sign of mourning, but I didn't see any of the desperation or profound anguish of burials at home, because for these people death was not the termination of a process, but something natural and inevitable.

It was my first trip to Nepal, and just a couple of days earlier a THAI airlines flight had crashed with 113 people on board. It was the autumn of 1992. To find myself with so much death, so close and in such an unexpected way, struck me as being a disturbing welcome, a disagreeable way to start the expedition. But, yet again, I know that **we live through things as we experience them from our own view of reality,** in my case, depending on the way in which we've been brought up.

In the West we're used to dealing with death with anguish and suffering. We reject it and hide it away. We even, on occasion, go to the extent of not telling a loved one that they are soon going to die.

In this part of the world, however, I discovered that the Buddhist and Hindu philosophies, which have much in common, take a different approach to death.

THE MOUNTAIN IS MY RELIGION

For Buddhism, burial is a transitory ritual in life, and death is a beginning which allows us to be reborn and to have another life. Lives go on repeating themselves one after the other so that we can continue to learn, little by little, until we acquire enough spiritual wisdom to reach Nirvana (a word I like). Then, once purified, no further reincarnations will be required.

Life is eternal, and death, necessary. This is not perceived as a tragedy; life is a preparation for death, and by eliminating fear, once we die we are assured of a good rebirth.

This means that Buddhist philosophy encourages one to live life to the full, enjoying it, because one is aware every second of **how short, wonderful and valuable** it is.

Listening to these concepts, I felt completely identified with them and was finally able to start putting into words the ideas which I had had when I was twenty-two but had never been able to express. This is similar to what happens when you listen to a song or read a poem, and you're astounded that someone has managed to put into words what you think but were unable to say. So that's how I felt as I learnt more about this philosophy and of the **need to enjoy the present at each passing moment.**

That is precisely what mountains give me, not that I feel I have to risk my life on them. It is simply the fact of being on them, doing sport in a relaxed fashion, or walking in some corner of the Pyrenees or in a Himalayan valley, that makes me feel surrounded by a feeling of my own smallness, the awareness of having taken advantage of each moment and not neglecting what I have. **Not wasting time on things that aren't worth it.** Perhaps I use the mountains as a tool to remind myself of the great, brief opportunity which existence provides. To a certain extent, the mountains are my religion, my philosophy.

I am not a follower of any of the existing religions, but that doesn't mean that I'm not a believer: I believe in nature, energy, spirituality; I believe in many things which don't necessarily have to express themselves through a god or gods. That is another aspect of Buddhism which attracted my attention. There is a coincidence between science and Buddhist philosophy which I like very much, and which agrees with Lavoisier's law of 1785, that states **"Nothing is lost, nothing is created, everything is transformed".** In the same way, one of the principles of Buddhism, which dates from the fifth century BCE, says that the mind, the awareness of conscious or unconscious phenomena, cannot be created or destroyed but rather is transformed by means of rebirth in another life.

Just as our bodies have to cope with a string of necessities that manifest themselves through hunger, tiredness or cold, our spiritual part, our soul, our spirit also has needs and if they are not satisfied, this may cause suffering.

There are as many ways of understanding spirituality as there are cultures or philosophical beliefs. Each person, it goes without saying, can find his or her own way of experiencing this spirituality, without the need or obligation to join or identify with any pre-established faith.

A project with three peculiarities

With all these ideas dancing about in my head, we left Kathmandu, sitting on the roof of an old, run-down bus full of receptacles containing various materials and which creaked over the potholes on a poorly repaired road.

I kept a firm hold on the luggage rack and smelt the humidity of the ground dampened by the monsoons. With my eyes closed, I listened to the noise of the villages through which we passed and took pleasure in the growing uncertainty I felt as we approached the mountain we wanted to climb: a peak with an altitude of over 8,000 meters, located in Tibet: the Shishapangma.

This expedition was different in several different ways:

• We didn't want to ascend via the normal route, but rather wanted to do so via a route that had been opened up two years ago by the great Polish and Swiss mountaineers EDGAR LORETAN, WOJCIECH KURTYKAI AND JEAN TROILLEti, whose feat had not been repeated. It was a more difficult, demanding and technically complex route than the others.

• We didn't want to ascend with the traditional system involving a weight-burdened expedition, with the help of porters, oxygen, fixed ropes, and pre-pitched camps. What we wanted was to take rucksacks that contained only what we needed, as if we were only going to spend a few days on the mountain. We wanted to do this in the nimblest, quickest and simplest way: in pure alpine style. We still hadn't made an ascent in this fashion in the Himalayas, but something inside us told us that this was the way we had to meet this particular challenge. This was the style that suited us best, with which we identified, and to do this any other way would have struck us as being uninteresting and unattractive.

• And one final detail, that wasn't that important, was that our average age was twenty-two. That meant there were a few doubts as regards our experience, on the part of the organisations we approached for funding for our expedition. But we were lucky enough to get the support of a group that shared our way of thinking: the sports department of the Polytechnic University of Catalonia, which had the courage to help us with this audacious project, simply because they trusted us and believed in us.

More than once I've heard it said that we alpine mountaineers are always putting our lives in danger, that we like taking risks. I would like to comment on those two points: **risk is one thing but danger is another thing altogether.**

Danger is a fact, whereas risk is to do with probability. Danger is something that can cause harm; risk is the possibility of harm in the future. Almost nobody in his or her right mind and with even a little self-esteem would consciously place themselves in danger, but, by contrast, risk is intrinsic to living and existing. It is probable that we will die, get ill, fall in love, or get a little thinner from the moment we get out of bed and place our feet on the floor. Often, it's the things that matter most which involve a certain amount of risk. A life without any kind of risk would have no surprises, no passion, and we would find it so emotionally dull that it could even put an end to our existence.

HOW TO REDUCE THE RISK FACTOR

Yes, for sure, there were dangers inherent in this expedition. But by identifying them, controlling them, and overcoming the fears and concerns that such fears could give rise to, we had the best tool possible when it came to dealing with our goals and facing up to new challenges. How? First by **identifying the dangers** and then **reducing the level of risk.**

Objective danger is all around us. In the mountains, a snow avalanche, falling stones, a crevasse, a serac, etc.

In order to reduce the risk of this objective danger we can use:

• **Information.** For example, by observing and knowing when the last snowfall was, how much snow fell, the angle of the slope, the temperatures, and the history and previous events that had taken place at any given point along the route.

• **Preparation.** Scaling techniques for both rock and ice, suitable material, training, theories and concepts which have to be borne in mind.

• **Experience.** This is as important as the other two things, and is something which can't be learnt or read about, but which is, on the contrary, personal and acquired over time. *Experience allows us to take advantage of fear.* It gives us a sixth sense, intuition, which makes you turn back when you see a particular type of cloud, when you can smell humidity in the wind, or when you notice something in the snow before an avalanche.

On the other hand, there are several subjective risks: those which, by contrast with the objective risks, affect each individual's personal circumstances and are difficult to define objectively. Such as, for example, tiredness, dehydration, a slip or a fall... **The minimisation of such risks depends on knowledge of our personal limits and on our honesty when it comes to setting our goals.**

Duracelli Segarra

There was absolutely nobody on the mountain when we arrived, and nobody turned up during the two months we were there. We didn't have any kind of communication with the outside world, other than the radios we used to speak to each other, which were powered only by AA batteries.

One day while we were making photos for our sponsors, we took out a Duracell rabbit from the ads that company was making at the time - in which a rabbit banged on a little drum - Duracell being our sponsor for the batteries. Then Xavi Lamas said:

—Look Araceli, they're like you, these Duracell batteries, they last and last and last...

That nickname stuck with me during the entire expedition. But I wasn't so sure that my batteries could cope with what lay ahead of us. We hadn't yet reached an altitude of 8,000 meters and I didn't have enough experience to know what would happen to my body at that height. Even so, of all the members of the group, I was the one that had climbed highest: to 7,200 meters. I was leading by a ridiculous difference of 40 meters.

Namaste!

One day when the weather was bad, I went into the kitchen to talk with Nima, our cook. He was a short, sturdy person like us, with dark skin, dark eyes and the look of a child. He was always smiling happily. When we played cards and he won the last hand, he would throw the card onto the table and wave his arm in the air, with a sense of joy that was catching.

I wanted to know what he thought, what he felt, what his opinions were. I was curious about his culture and his religion. He told me he came from a very poor family, from a remote rural village.

Nepal is one of the poorest countries in the world. 30% of its inhabitants live below the poverty line and survive on just 10 euros a month. 80% of the population live in rural areas in which there no medical services, education, or proper hygiene.

Despite this poverty, when you arrive in Nepal, and even more so when you cross the rice paddies, the villages, and the mountains where people are poorer still, when you enter a house for a cup of tea and eat some biscuits, you don't sense the misery, uneasiness or anguish that any of us would feel if we lived in such conditions. People smile, sing, dance, play and make jokes.

The Nepalese porters carry loads such as wooden beams, doors, or boxes full of cans of Coca-Cola along mountain paths where there are no proper roads. As they do so, they greet you in passing with a *Namaste!*[4] And smile at you. And they *all* do that, like Nima.

The rationale behind this way of facing up to life, behind this happy, joyous attitude, comes, yet again, from their philosophy, which makes them live every moment to the utmost and makes them aware that they cannot choose their own circumstances. Which is why they try to make the best of them as they possibly can.

THE ULTIMATE FREEDOM OF EVERY HUMAN BEING

We can choose how we want to respond to any given circumstances and our happiness will depend on this response, which we and only we can decide on. So **our happiness doesn't depend on chance, on having been born rich or poor, tall or short, or if it's raining or if it's sunny, if there's a stain on my skirt or if the guy at the petrol station is in a lousy mood.** Our happiness depends on our choice.

[4] A greeting which originated in India and is used to say 'Hello' or 'Goodbye'. Literally, it means: 'I revere you'.

Although this idea is easy enough to describe, it's difficult to put into practice. The first step, and sometimes the most difficult one, is to be aware that **we are facing a situation in which we can decide which response to give.** And the next step, which the first few times is also difficult, involves changing this response. Once we are aware of this we can put it into practice, and practice makes perfect. Over time, we'll be able to change our attitude effortlessly, or it might simply change on the spot.

Viktor Frankl, the creator of logotherapy and the author of *Man's Search for Meaning,* had this to say about the matter: **"Everything can be taken from a man except one thing: the last of the human freedoms - to choose one's attitude in any given set of circumstances, to choose one's way."**

The magnet of uncertainty

On this expedition we allowed ourselves to be guided by instinct and the little experience we had at age twenty-two. Even so we never left **preparation, training, documentation, strategy and a disposition to be flexible** to chance. They were our best tools when it came to balancing what we had with what we were lacking.

We made sure that our enthusiasm didn't get out of hand: enthusiasm can be good when needed and dangerous when it isn't.

Our initial plan had to be corrected on more than one occasion due to our doubts about the state of the snow, the unpredictability of the climate and the effects of exhaustion.

After having acclimatised ourselves to the surrounding peaks, and feeling that we were finally ready, we headed straight for our main goal. When we launched the assault on the summit, we faced an unwelcoming, unexplored wall without any kind of ready-prepared equipment.

So, what was it that made us want to climb, and what made us dare to do it? Well, just this: **the uncertainty, the magnetic attraction of not knowing what's going to happen or what we're going to find.**

UNCERTAINTY AND APPREHENSION

Uncertainty is often presented to us as something to be feared, instead of being something that we can relish when it appears. How can we work better than we usually do with uncertainty?

1. By not having any great expectations. If we expect something really good is going to happen, and it doesn't, we feel disappointed. And if we expect something really bad, we are focussing on everything in a negative way and that means that things are not going to turn out well. The best thing we can do is to put all our efforts into our project, working actively to achieve our aims.

2. Be ready to be flexible.

We can prepare different plans, but we still don't know what's going to end up happening and what we're going to have to do given the circumstances. We'll have to improvise and make new plans based on what we've improvised. Flexibility and a predisposition to adapt ourselves are the key.

Uncertainty can lead to fear and distress. That will block us mentally and make us physically tense; our blood pressure will be altered and that can tire and exhaust us. **A little meditation or visualisation can help us to relax so that we can handle any uncertainty in a better way.**

If there's something you think that you can do - a little bit of preparation, an adjustment etc. - do it and don't think about it again.

Enjoy what's happening in the moment, without thinking about what's going to happen two days later, and don't get fixated about what happened the day before yesterday. What matters, what you are in control of, what you can touch and enjoy, is in the present. The rest doesn't exist.

One of the dangers of uncertainty is that of falling into the trap of worrying too much, something which fills us with anguish and can eventually paralyse us. We're afraid of what we don't know, but according to research by a team of American psychologists...

- 40% of the things we worry about don't end up happening.

- 30% of our worries are to do with decisions that have already been made and which we cannot change.

- 12% are to do with other people's acts, which don't depend on us.

- 10% are to do with our health, which we do have to look after, but not worry about, as the only thing that will do is make it worse.

- Only 8% of the other things about which we are worried are really worth worrying about.

The calm before the storm

After having spent a little over a month acclimatising ourselves, we delayed the assault on the mountain, because I was completely exhausted when I reached the foot of the wall at 5,30 meters, having lugged a rucksack that was too heavy for me over the ten kilometers from Base Camp.

We had minimum amount of provisions, but that wasn't a cause for alarm. We simply reckoned that we could adapt ourselves to that situation.

I spent that whole day of rest rationing the food, stretched out in the tent on a sleeping bag, without any books, without music, just staring at the ceiling which was yellow and warm and let the daylight in while the sun heated up the tent to the point where it got stuffy. I rested comfortably, I'd even say I felt happy, but above all proud to belong to a group which had delayed the ascent for a day because of me.

I had got very tired, on the way to the foot of that wall. I remember that every few steps I had to stop, I couldn't lug the weight of that rucksack for more than a hundred meters at a time. My neck, shoulders, lumbar region and my entire body was complaining and refused to go on. I stopped very five minutes, until I reached the spot where I was now lying in the tent.

It was there that I remembered the obstinacy with which I went canoeing, concentrating my eyes on one specific point. I paddled blindly, with more energy than I really had, without bearing in mind that my fellow canoer was sixteen and I was just nine. Paddling determinedly, concentrating on not losing my pace, and on keeping time with my colleague in that race, without doubting or even thinking that I wasn't suited to that contest, without prejudices, without shame, which is the only way a child can live through any situation.

I often think that we shouldn't lose this child-like way of thinking, which allows us not to doubt, not to feel ashamed, not to stick labels on ourselves. I now faced up to this mountain with the same stubbornness and obstinacy, without thinking about whether or not I was suited to this challenge. That day I had just one aim in mind: to recover fully and to continue the trip the next day.

The final assault

And that's what I did, carrying a slightly lighter load, when we started the final assault. Without fixed ropes we took on that snowy, icy wall with its 45 degree slope.

Surprisingly, we got there fairly smoothly and set up the only camp possible which that all but vertical wall allowed us to. For reasons of space and safety we couldn't have set it up anywhere else. The mountain gave the orders, and we had to decide if wanted to play along or not.

That night, the night of the assault on the summit, I felt a strange calmness. It's odd, but I wasn't at all nervous, and the reason is that I completely trusted the people around me and also my own abilities.

EXPANDING ONE'S OWN LIFE

When you're on a mountain, confidence - as in so many other aspects of life - is essential in order to bring the project to a satisfactory close; it's an indispensable ingredient. In this project, everyone needed to feel confidence in the ability of all the others. It could never have been planned, initiated, or developed if that confidence hadn't existed. Not one of us would have got involved. This delicate yet sturdy edifice, so to speak, would not have remained standing.

When we set out the basic plan at the beginning, when we worked out the details of the project, while we looked for funding or when we made alterations to our strategy, if that confidence hadn't been there, the whole team or an important part of it would have backed out.

Confidence shapes our lives and determines our possibilities, both collectively and individually. As the writer Anaïs Nin said: **"Life shrinks or expands in proportion to one's courage."**

We left at night and went along that corridor in almost total darkness, once again without ropes. Step by step, adding up the meters. Each metre that went over our personal record was a milestone for us.

We were all happy after we'd reached 7,200 meters. We scaled 1,300 meters of uneven slope until we reached the central peak of Shishapangma, at 8,008 meters, climbing non-stop for fourteen hours.

Our first 8,000, for Ernest, Albert, Ferran and me. Up there we were small, fragile, tiny and so very puny, seen from the peak of a mountain that was so big and so powerful that I felt I was losing my grip and might vanish into thin air. From up there we could see the Tibetan plateau that had been hidden behind the mountain.

I engraved it all in my head. I didn't want to lose one single detail of that wonder, of that moment. But almost all visual memories are lost eventually, and what remain are the other memories, the feelings that we feel in our guts rather than storing them in our heads. Memories, for me, of wanting to take advantage of every moment and knowing that yesterday didn't matter anymore, that I would live to see tomorrow, and that now, now only, what I was doing at this precise instant was the only thing that mattered.

The descent, which took two days, was pretty complicated. Not having any fixed ropes to grasp onto when tired or when we got lost in the storm that hit us as we were going down, made everything a lot more demanding. But we finally made it without any harm done. We got back a little thinner than before, that was all.

CHANGING YOUR MINDSET

After that first 8,000 metre summit, I realised that the greatest obstacle we overcame wasn't the mountain itself, not its particular features and technical difficulties, nor was it anything to do with our having prepared ourselves thoroughly for the trip, in order to make up for our lack of experience.

The greatest obstacle was to do with changing our mindset, breaking paradigms, both ours and those of the people around us. By planning the project in a different, new, and for some people crazy way. We had to abandon a certain way of thinking.

A paradigm is a preconceived, and well-established idea which we often don't question and which can limit, to a great extent, our potential, our development and what we can achieve, because our ideas are decisive when it comes to achieving our results.

From a historical perspective, the physicist Max Planck said that **"A new scientific truth does not triumph by convincing its opponents and making them see the light, but rather because its opponents eventually die, and a new generation grows up that is familiar with it."**

As far as our lives are concerned, we are not aware that we have paradigms. Sometimes they are ideas that we take for granted. Sometimes we haven't even chosen them ourselves: they can be imposed on us by our society and culture. That the Earth is flat, that women can't carry out certain tasks, etc.... are some of the paradigms which needed to be broken or are currently being broken.

Realising that we have them is, perhaps, the most difficult part, because it's often difficult for us to be aware of them and to recognise them for what they are. To break with them is up to us. If a concept limits us and doesn't work for us, maybe it's time to consider abandoning it.

Innovation is often the result of strange, crazy or unorthodox ideas, or so they seem at first sight. Himalayism, the alpine style which we had recently discovered and employed successfully, was nothing if not innovative. And the basis for making crazy proposals without fear of being judged or marginalised is, once again, confidence. The confidence we shared when it came to saying crazy things, the courage to make proposals without being afraid that we'd no longer be treated in the same way or would be looked at askance, and the confidence shown in us by the university team that supported us when it came to carrying out this project.

The wheel of fortune

When we got back to Kathmandu, the same way we'd come, on the roof of a bus, we found out that another aeroplane had crashed. It was a PIA flight, with 167 passengers, just 59 days after the THAI one. Two days after this accident, my brother Roger had landed in Kathmandu on a PIA flight. I didn't know he'd come and found him by chance that same day, walking around in a city of one and a half million inhabitants.

MAKING GOOD LUCK WORK FOR YOU

There is luck and there are coincidences. Running into a person in a particular place, taking one plane and not another, a tile that falls off a roof, a stray bullet... Everything is a game of chance which we cannot control. When it comes down to it, we are not 100% in charge when it comes to staying alive.

But I also believe that you can create your own luck, and take advantage of the opportunities that life offers you. We are not the puppets of fortune, nor can we blame everything bad that happens to us on chance. Nor can we blame our genetics (by saying, for example, "I'm too short, and that's why no one'll give me a job"), or blame the circumstances around us ("I'm unhappy because my boss is insufferable and my girlfriend never stops nagging me"). We are all more or less lucky. What matters is if we can recognise that, take advantage of it, and improve our luck.

The Canadian economist Stephen Leacock once said: **"I am a great believer in luck, and the harder I work the more I have of it"**.

Four years after this expedition, in a base camp I would meet an American who wanted to make a documentary. And a year later, at eight in the evening, I would be catching a plane from JLF airport to Paris.

Thirty minutes later, another plane, which had taken off just two gates along from mine, at the same airport and that was also flying to Paris, exploded in mid-air twelve minutes after take-off, with 230 people on board. For eight hours, David, who'd dropped me off at the airport, thought I was dead.

V. Mistakes, Squabbles and Other Stuff.

Remember, upon the conduct of each depends the fate of all.
ALEXANDER THE GREAT

I was running, out of control, through the darkness of that moonless forest. I was going as fast as I could, in a life and death race, sweating, out of breath, something which forced me to stop from time to time to just manage to swallow some saliva while my heart beat frantically.

The light from the torch gave off sharp blows of light from side to side, like a *Star Wars* lightsabre. At the speed I was going I couldn't see where I was putting my feet, which stumbled over branches or stones from time to time, making me do a grotesque dance, like that of a little bird learning to land, nearly breaking its neck, but at the last moment it manages to stay upright.

Too fast to handle all the information coming at me at once, I suddenly saw him hiding behind a thicket. Without stopping, I called out:

"I've got him!"

And, without realising what I was doing, I jumped from the top of some rocks and fell straight into a bramble.

"Ouch, shit!!"

I didn't say a word more. The head of Lluís, the monitor who we had to capture during that night-time gymkhana, reared up from the grass, and he made a slight movement of his head that indicated both surprise and displeasure, and went to look for some help to get me out of there.

Meanwhile, I stayed where I was, quiet as a mouse, not budging an inch, feeling the jabs from the thorns all over my body, which no longer hurt. Stretched out, looking at the firmament, I saw the stars which pricked the sky, not letting through enough light from the luminous world which I was sure must have been on the other side of that dark fabric.

I was twelve, and the summer camps were the best thing that happened to me in that season.

When they took me out, I was scratched and bleeding just about everywhere: legs, arms, hands and face. When I got to the camp, the cook, who was also the nurse, exclaimed:

"Heavens, Araceli, you've done it again!"

Last summer, playing the handkerchief game, I'd run so fast so that nobody could take the handkerchief from me, and ended up in another bramble, but that time the nettles were a little less unpleasant. An incredible feeling, like an electric current, ran through my body and made me curious as to what it really was, for the whole of the rest of the afternoon, which was as long as it lasted. Every time I stamped on the ground, a kind of itching crept up my legs, started burning at the height of the quadriceps femoris and then vanished.

Deciding emotionally

There I was, jumping the gun, yet again. That's what I did with the friendly and understanding Iberia stewardess who looked at me disapprovingly from the other side of the tourist class check-in counter at Barcelona airport. I'd just signed a Visa receipt for 2000€ for excess luggage.

There are situations which we let get the better of us and which we don't know how to deal with properly. Stress can make us act hastily, without choosing the best possible option and our emotions end up having a direct influence on our decisions. Paying 2000€ wasn't exactly the way I'd wanted to resolve the situation, and for sure there were countless other possible solutions and much better decisions than the one I'd taken in order to solve that particular dilemma.

But our creativity works better when we're not under pressure. To end up making the correct decision, or to bear in mind all the possible options, doesn't usually happen when we feel harried and are forced to make a quick decision.

DECIDING WITHOUT PRESSURE AND UNDER PRESSURE

What I should have done was leave the queue and stop arguing with that person. That way, I would have avoided the unpleasant feeling of being stared at by the other people who urgently wished me to respond and act fast, because there was quite a queue. The most efficient procedure would have been to follow these three steps:

* FIRST: to calmly outline and identify the problem. If it's not a matter of life or death, we shouldn't allow anyone to hurry us. They're the ones in a hurry, not us.

* SECOND: take a look at some or all possibilities and search for options: no matter how absurd they might seem – leave some material on the floor, haggle, ask to speak to the person in charge, delay the flight, upgrade to business class, make out that you're having a heart attack...

* THIRD: take the decision that's going to make you feel better, the one you think is the most coherent, and, above all, the decision which is going to leave you with the least bad taste in your mouth.

But I didn't do any of that. I behaved as we usually do when we have to decide under pressure and our emotions get in the way: rushing ahead without looking at our options.

Such is the least efficient procedure that we can follow in these cases:

* FIRST: you get panicky, confused and in a bad mood, which affects your emotional state.

* SECOND: you reckon the only option is the first one you come across. In this particular case, the one suggested by the friendly stewardess, which happened to be the most convenient one for the airline, but the least favourable for me.

* THIRD: you make a decision based on the only option in sight.

To put a rapid end to that nightmare, in an increasingly bad mood I paid a sum of money which would have upgraded me to business class, but I was obliged to fly in tourist class. Far from feeling satisfied at having solved that bothersome incident and then moving on, I ended up feeling frustrated, irritated and upset. Not just because I'd unexpectedly had to overspend my budget, but because I hadn't been able to cope properly. In theory, I was somebody who had been trained to make important decisions (sometimes regarding matters of life or death) in complicated situations (hanging from a wall 800 meters from the ground or on a snowy slope at an altitude of 8,000 meters) and this time I'd allowed my emotions to make the decision for me.

THE GOOD SIDE OF BAD DECISIONS

We need to think clearly and lucidly in order to make good decisions yet even so, our actions are more influenced by our emotions and intuition than we think. When our emotions are affected, often in a negative way (being very much in love could also be an example of being emotionally affected) they muddle our thinking and our ability to judge correctly. Often we are not aware of the role these emotions play when it comes to decision-making. If we realise on the spot that our emotions have started to befuddle our thinking then that's a first step towards controlling the situation.

The good thing about having made rushed emotional decisions is that it helps us not to make the same mistake in the future. Apropos of this, there's a modern fable – the author is unknown – which tells us about a journalist who visited the president of a bank to ask him the following question:

"Sir, what is the secret of your success?"

"Two words."

"Really? Which ones?"

"Good decisions."

"And how do you manage to make good decisions?"

"One word."

"Which one, sir?"

"Experience."

"And how does one get experience?"

"Two words".

"So, what are they?"

"Bad decisions".

The enchanted forest

It wasn't a great start. Even so, days later we would reach the solitary Base Camp on our mountain: the Kangchenjunga. With its 8,585 meters, it's the third highest mountain in the world.

The approach walk to Base Camp was one of the most naturally wild that I've ever taken, thanks to the luxuriance, the density and the humidity of its forests, in which rhododendrons, far from being the little ones we see close to home, are huge, tall trees. If you want to smell their dew and fleshy flowers you have to stick your neck into the air. You feel like Alice in Wonderland, made small in a gigantic world with trees, mountains and rivers of huge dimensions. You are about to live a wonderful adventure in the middle of an outlandish world whose history is yet to be written.

It was a nebulous jungle wrapped in moss that hung from the forest trees, that looked as if it had been painted with a few brush strokes by a capricious Impressionist painter; sometimes it was greenish or yellowing or ochre. As if someone had drawn moustaches on trees which reached up the mountain to altitudes of over 3,000 meters.

On some days we had to climb over high ground with over a thousand meters' distance between tall, endless stony paths and the roaring of hidden waterfalls. At the end of the day, we were soaked in sweat and humidity, and exhausted. Then we would eat the local food in the humble, smoked-wood houses of the native inhabitants, who welcomed us with amusement and curiosity, as in this region tourists were scarce or non-existent.

Arrival at Base Camp

Having to discuss a settlement with our porters, who had gone on strike, broke the idyllic spell of the approach walk and probably set in motion a string of events which would end up having an effect on the final result of the project.

When we reached a Base Camp, normally the porters would set down their loads. Then the *sirdar* – the porters' boss – would pay them and they'd leave more or less quickly, depending on how far away they were from some small village, or how long their return journey was.

In this case, they rushed off, and once again we were left on our own in the middle of a glacier with a heap of supply canisters, haul bags containing various materials and crates of food :enough things for us to slowly set up our refuge for the next couple of months.

I was surprised at how clean Base Camp was, without a trace of the remains of other expeditions. Having said which, it wasn't all that strange. Ours was the only expedition, and each year there was rarely more than one.

The longest night

The following day Héctor and I went out to reconnoitre the terrain a bit. We wanted to see where we had to cross the glacier, avoiding crevasses and blocks, looking for the best path with which to start the route. The rest of the team, an international group that had joined up with us to share expenses, stayed at Base Camp to finish setting up the kitchen.

We weren't expecting to spend much time out, so all we were carrying was a little water, a folding screen, a rope, ice axes, and crampons.

After an hour, we found a more or less practical passage along which we could cross over to the other side of the glacier, but the entry point to the mountain was tricky. So we went up the glacier to see if the wall had a weaker spot somewhere.

Bit by bit, we went on crossing crevasses, and moved by the vastness, calmness and solitude of the place, we continued climbing without realising how much time had gone by. When we decided to turn back, because beyond where we were there couldn't possibly be a potential entrance to the route, we decided to head back through the inside of the glacier.

We walked in a circle so as to explore new options, and then things started getting more complicated. A sharp blow threw me to the ground. The rope had tensed and Héctor had fallen into a crevasse hidden by the snow. He got out at once, without any damage done, and without having lost a single ice axe, but that incident meant that we had to go slower.

The chaos of ice and crevasses that faced us on the way down as darkness approached, complicated our return considerably. Without us realising, night had caught up with us.

Without headlamps, our only option was to stop. We took refuge in a little cave we found, full of stalactites against which I bumped my head while we jumped up and down to lessen the cold in which I was beginning to freeze. A trickle of blood ran down my forehead to remind me that I was still alive, but maybe I needed to change tactics.

I remained on the same spot, marching like a soldier but without moving forward. I did that, trying to warm myself up a little and with a trembling jaw, for maybe three hours.

It was two in the morning, we were at an altitude of more than 6,000 meters in the middle of a Himalayan glacier and all I had was a thermal shirt and a folding screen. The cold was biting into me, and from time to time I gave cries that were muffled by desperation. I would have to last out until seven o'clock, when there would be enough light to go on walking. But I didn't think that with the clothes I was wearing and in that cold, I could stand five more hours.

I've always heard it said that dying of cold is gentle and peaceful: "white death", they call it. Maybe that's the case if you're wearing a down jacket, but I can assure you that if you're wearing thin clothes, it hurts and makes you furious! What an idiotic way to die!

Suddenly, from behind a mountain, the only thing that could get us out of there made an unexpected appearance: the moon! There it was, lighting up the night, bouncing its glimmer off the snow and amplifying it as if it were a lighthouse. We rushed out, at first with our legs and the rest of our bodies stiff with cold, but after a short while we were walking at a steady pace, crossing our fingers that we wouldn't make any mistakes and fall into another crevasse.

A few meters from Base Camp, we met a team that had come out to look for us. After the doctor had stitched my head up, we went to sleep just as it started to get light. My teeth were still chattering. It was six in the morning. In fact, I'd been mistaken: I'd only have had to have lasted four more hours...I still think I wouldn't have made it.

And what are we going to do now?

I took several days to recover, while the other team set off to mark the route along the path we'd found. The start of the wall was a little complicated, but it was the only possible entry point we'd found after going over the entire glacier.

It took us two days to reach Camp I. Once again, tricky terrain slowed us up, and this time we were laden with tents, food, clothes and headlamps. We had to set up the tent and spend the night at the foot of the ice wall, until, the next day, we managed to reach Camp I, which was located on a highly visible ridge.

About halfway through the expedition, one day when we were returning to Base Camp, coming down from Camp I, one of our colleagues went to take a look some distance away from our route and found remains of cans and other waste. In fact, he'd discovered the real Base Camp, which was located in a comfortable corner with grass and earth, on one side of the glacier.

In which case, where had we installed ourselves? By mistake, we'd gone much lower down, right in the middle of the glacier, far from what should have been our real Base Camp.

That explained plenty of things which had at first surprised us. We hadn't taken much notice of them, when in fact they were very important. The fact that Base Camp was so clean, without any remains from previous expeditions, that the porters were in such a hurry to rush off and leave us in the middle of a glacier, that the access to the route was so complicated...None of that fitted in with the path to Camp I. Maybe we'd opened up a new by-pass.

"And what we going to do now?" we asked ourselves. I think the best thing would have been to correct the situation, no matter how tough and difficult that might have been. If you don't correct a basic error, there'll always be a faultline in the cement holding together the project, which could end up affecting the entire structure.

We could have struck camp and in two days we would have taken everything we had to the new location. And while we were on the mountain, the cook and his assistant would have brought all the food. After all, we were a lightweight expedition. We weren't carrying oxygen and we'd already fixed the little rope we were carrying in place. So why didn't we correct our mistake? Why did we go on climbing starting at the false base camp, when it was obvious that the route from there was tougher and harder?

Between staying at the false base camp and taking the longer and more complicated route, or striking camp and spending two or three days making the move to the real base camp in exchange for making our route shorter, why didn't we seriously consider the second option?

WHEN YOUR PRIDE COMMITS HARA-KIRI

Why is it so difficult to accept that we're wrong? We often think as well as feel that we're right. We were quite happy in our Base Camp and that wasn't a problem. We didn't think we'd made a mistake, but we had. It's at the moment you realise you have, that you feel badly, often even ashamed and humiliated. Because in this case, let's not forget it, even though the porters had left us in the middle of the glacier, there where they and the *sirdar* had told us Base Camp was, the bottom line was that the responsibility for knowing where it really was and deciding where to install ourselves, was ours and ours alone. It was us who were unable to pinpoint exactly where Base Camp really was.

Sometimes we have a "tendency to confirm". That is to say, we intentionally seek out information that supports our beliefs and reject anything to the contrary. We chase after clues, proofs, evidence that we're doing the right thing and not the opposite. That helps us to ignore certain facts which otherwise would have helped us to correct our mistakes in time, no matter how much of an effort that might have taken, instead of us losing our way.

Quino, the Argentinian thinker and cartoonist, through his sarcastic character Mafalda, said: "When you admit you're wrong, that's when your pride commits hara-kiri".

A deadly fright

Héctor, a member of the team, and I climbed up one day to set up Camp II. We were laden with ropes and it was sunny. We went down the great plateau, after having crossed a broken, labyrinthine serac which we'd spent all of yesterday trying to work out where it led.

We were roped together as we walked, but the terrain was new to us and there were crevasses. When we reached the slope we attached new ropes while Héctor, now untied, went on ahead, faster than the rest of the team, along an open ridge. Everything that happened from that point on has stayed in my memory ever since.

I couldn't catch up with him as he was going too fast, so I let him go ahead as I had many other times. I watched him out of the corner of my eye. I saw that he took off his rucksack and attached himself to the only rope he had left, which was fifteen meters long. I was carrying the rest of the ropes. He knelt down and drove a half-metre stake into the snow. Then he immediately began crawling on all fours so as to spread his body weight over the fragile surface he wanted to cross.

My heartbeat accelerated. It wouldn't have been a problem for him to have waited a little until we'd reached him and ensured he was properly attached...

Suddenly, my fears were realised. I saw Héctor sink into the snow-covered crevasse that he'd been trying to cross. He fell head first into the gap and I saw his feet go under. Thinking quickly, trying to keep calm, I told myself: "He'll be fine, he's roped up and he's thrust a stake into the snow."

I watched as the rope slithered fast over the ground and was swallowed up by the crevasse like a piece of spaghetti. The rope tensed and the stake was pulled out.

—

NooooooooooooooooooooooooooooooooooooooooooooooooooAaaaaaaaaaa aaaaaaaaaaaaaaaaaaaaaaaaaaa!

It was the most breathless, anguished cry I had ever given in my life.

I knew that Héctor was dead. I couldn't breathe, I couldn't move, I couldn't think. My heart was beating hard and fast against my chest, as if I were suffocating.

"No, please, this can't be happening... No, please."

I tried to move quickly over to the crevasse, but I was a long way away. I couldn't run. We were at a high altitude: some 6,500 meters, and we weren't acclimatised.

An unexpected ending

Ten minutes later, a colleague got there before me. From a distance, he called out that Héctor was alive, that he'd heard him call from the darkness of the crevasse.

I remembered some stories I'd heard about Pakistani porters in the Baltoro valley and how after falling into one of the crevasses on the glacier during the approach walk, they'd become embedded in there without being able to move and had died of hypothermia before they could be taken out, in the cases when that was possible.

I tried not to think about that. Being negative wasn't going to help. When I got there, we finished setting up a rope and then let it fall into the crevasse.

After a little while, I saw that it had tensed and recognised the gentle rhythmic movement of someone who is coming up with the help of a rope. I was overcome by emotion and my legs gave way underneath me. I burst out crying.

When his head appeared, his goggles were askew, but aside from having lost one of his ski poles, he was unharmed. Luckily, he'd landed right in the middle of a snow bridge more than twenty meters further down, cushioned by the mattress of snow that had fallen into the crevasse with him. If he'd fallen a little more to the left or right he would have been thrown who knew how many meters further down.

He sat down on the snow, I wiped my tears away and went up to give him a kiss and a hug. He smiled playfully and said:

"Well, now we know we can't go through here; we'll have to take another route."

"Go to hell!" I answered back, crossly.

And I sat down on my rucksack, watching how the other two went on opening up the route while I tried to calm myself. At least I had the consolation of knowing I wasn't the only one who liked to rush ahead.

A RUBBER BAND ABOUT TO SNAP

Rushing or being in a hurry usually has dreadful consequences. Even the most professional of experts can make this mistake. Sometimes it's just in our nature to want to do things as fast as possible; at others, we simply want time to be on our side.

Trying to take short cuts can force us to redo all our work, or can even end up with us getting hurt. A useful tool is **to think about the consequences of rushing things**. That can make us take things more in our stride. As the Spanish saying goes: "Dress me slowly, I'm in a hurry."

In his book *In Praise of Slowness: Challenging The Cult of Speed,* the Canadian journalist Carl Honoré assures us that **"Speed is not always the best policy.** Evolution works on the principle of survival of the fittest, not the fastest. Remember who won the race between the tortoise and the hare. **As we hurry through life, cramming more into every hour, we are stretching ourselves to the breaking point [like a rubber band]."**

A high altitude restaurant.

Just as we'd done on other expeditions, I was in charge of the food supply. It's a job I very much enjoy doing: I try to find foodstuffs that will be surprising, amusing and that will cheer up the whole team. For our group of three, I prepared everything that would function as high altitude food, none of which was available in Kathmandu: various energy bars, sachets of dehydrated foods such as purées, wild mushrooms, fruit, couscous, algae and dried meats, powdered energy drinks, coffee, cappuccinos, chocolate with low sugar levels, vitamin supplements, etc. And for Base Camp, I prepared a few delicacies to break the monotony of rice or pasta dinners. Not very many, because they were for the entire expedition: a total of eight people.

I nearly left this food behind. It was part of the excess baggage whose weight I had had to pay in gold: a menu to be consumed at 5,500 meters for the same price as a five star Michelin restaurant:

—First course: Seafood purée (from a sachet) with sautéed prawns (from a tin). e
—Second course: Duck confit (from a tin) with caramelised onion (canned).
—Dessert: Yoghurt cake (from a sachet) and After Eight
—To drink: red wine from the Ribero del Duero region.

A bag of toasted sweet corn

One day, while we rested at Camp II after having lugged up a load of material, I was lying down inside the tent. There was bright sunlight and not the slightest of breezes. I stayed there, lolling around and half asleep, what with tiredness and the heat which had been building up inside.

Suddenly, one of the group entered and with him came the smell of what we called *kikos* – fried and salted sweet corn -. I lifted my head a little to sniff it and then let it fall back onto the jacket which was serving as a pillow. I held my breath for a moment and then, my lips pressed together and my eyes open, I thought: "I'm starting to get a cerebral oedema".

This is one of the ways in which they begin: visual aural, olfactive and other hallucinations. I'd forgotten to bring any *kikos*, although it's one of the things I prefer the most at a high altitude. So I believed I was smelling something that I didn't think existed.

I remember a colleague on one expedition who got stuck in a tent at 7000 meters, thanks to a storm. On the second or third day, they radioed her to ask her how she was, and she replied that she was just fine, and was playing cards with the Sherpas. She was starting to get an oedema which, fortunately, disappeared when she manged to come back down.

Suddenly, I realised that that couldn't have been my case. We'd only spent a couple of hours up here and oedemas only manifest themselves after twenty-four hours. So it couldn't be an oedema. The only other option was that the *kikos* were real. By observing closely I discovered that, indeed, there was someone who had some. He'd left the tent and was eating them without anybody else being able to see what he had brought for his own private consumption. Like that, he wouldn't have to share them.

I felt deeply disappointed: I believed we were all working together to achieve a common objective, and that we were all committed to this 100%. I personally gave and offered everything I had, whereas here was someone who was keeping his personal parcel just for himself. He had received, but would not share.

SELF-ESTEEM AND GENEROSITY

Selfish behaviour is like a seed that, once germinated, can end up disrupting a group and splintering it. It's an attitude which, once the others have discovered it, can prevent them from working together and making a collective effort, to the extent that they will eventually work only in their own interests, thus weakening the group.

A team requires that its efforts complement each other, so that 1+1=3. Selfishness separates and sets apart the bonds between people. It's possible for a separated team to achieve its objective, but it will have many more options and energy if it's united.

We're talking about the kind of attitude which is the exact opposite of the one we mentioned in chapter 2, in which generosity is the basic, essential component when it comes to ensuring a group's cohesion. Whereas generosity is noble at heart, selfishness is a symptom of insecurity.

The psychotherapist and writer Nathaniel Branden made a direct link between generosity and self-esteem. In his own words: **"There is overwhelming evidence that the higher the level of self-esteem, the more likely one will be to treat others with respect, kindness, and generosity."**

From which it follows that selfish and inconsiderate individuals may well have a deeply ingrained insecurity which prevents them from giving, and giving of themselves, to others.

The day of the summit

In the end, on this expedition the group didn't really get on very well, quite the contrary, and this culminated in the well-known technique of tailgating. This is a manoeuvre which, unfortunately, I've seen only too often in the Himalayas, but also in other professions.

The most egregious example of this took place towards the end of the project, when we were about to make our definitive assault on the summit.

Martin, Héctor and I had gone on ahead all day, opening up a trail and finding the definitive path among the upper seracs. We slept at Camp III, while a Polish man, his Portuguese colleague and a Swiss man did the same, a few meters further up. We'd agreed that on the following morning they would go ahead of us, to open up the trail further. It was their turn.

The surprise came when, once we got up to their tents in the small hours, we couldn't see any signs of a trail. As the weather was bad, we supposed they had gone ahead and that the snow had made them invisible. A little later, we discovered that they were behind us. They'd waited for us to pass before leaving their tents.

Every time we stopped to get our breath back, they did the same. In this way, they never caught up with us.

The most surprising thing of all was that on top of this the Pole had oxygen bottles, which made it easier for him to walk, and move faster in a more relaxed way.

A few meters from the spot where we had to pitch Camp IV, they were finally obliged to join us and open up the trail as far as the rimaye where we'd set up the tent, at 7,900 meters.

We had a bad night. Not so much from the altitude, but more from the bad mood which that situation had given rise to. Too tired to reach the summit, we stayed on to rest for another day, while the other three moved their camp a hundred meters further up. I don't know if they didn't head for the summit because they were tired or because we hadn't gone ahead to open up the trail.

Twenty-four hours later, on the day we were to reach the summit, the weather was foul. It was snowing and the camp was blocked. You couldn't see anything, we didn't have any weather forecast or communication with the outside world. That was the price we paid for having a limited budget. Even so, we got out and started climbing.

When the weather started to clear, Héctor and I had gone past the place where the others had pitched their tents but we couldn't see them clearly; we decided to go back down. It was impossible for us to find the path and thus to reach the summit. What's more, there were no fixed ropes from here until Camp III.

We were surrounded by sheer mountainside, meaning that in a storm like the one we were in, we could easily fall into the void.

It didn't take us long to decide to head back but it took us quite a while to climb down. The snow from the plateau below reached up to our waists, and for just the two of us to open up a trail at that altitude was exhausting.

When we finally got to Camp III, I keeled over, saddened and drained of energy. Héctor too.

A few hours later, we heard on the radio that the others had reached the summit and were already returning to Camp IV. Quite simply, after having seen the weather conditions against which we'd fought and the time we had apparently taken to go up and climb back down, that struck me as incredible. Their descent was nothing short of *epic*.

We collected our material while the other team went off, each on his own, without paying any attention to anyone else.

PRECAUTIONS AGAINST SHAMELESS PEOPLE

In this group there was never any kind of confrontation, quarrel or argument. Maybe that was the big mistake. When, at certain moments, we started to notice little differences when it came to carrying out certain tasks, we should have made an issue of it, so that we could hold talks, and speak.

We gave them a wide berth, thinking that in this way we could avoid any unpleasant scenes, but the opposite happened. Similar behaviour to theirs, typical of shameless people, can be found in other fields.

There follows a series of measures that can help us to control this kind of situation:

1. It's vital to identify any given problem as soon as it arises, and not to let any more time go by than is strictly necessary.

2. Shameless people have highly developed skills when it comes to taking advantage of others, to the extent that even those who are at the receiving end of their abuse, don't realise it. So it's important to make it clear what the limits, objectives and expectations of the group are, and to stick firmly to them.

3. There are certain attitudes which make certain people an easy target for shameless people, who can sniff out their weaknesses and take advantage of them. In order to avoid this...

-We shouldn't feel bad about having certain expectations about other people.

-We shouldn't think we are responsible for the entire group.

188

-We shouldn't always try and keep other people happy, even at our own expense.

-We mustn't accept poor input with sentences like. "Well, look, at least that's something."

-Teamwork has to involve everybody, not only one or two people.

A final conclusion

During this expedition we made a few mistakes, many of which could have been avoided. Even so, later I would experience other errors, because learning consists of making mistakes, thinking about them, and letting them teach us something. Mistakes which, in the end, will be instructive and useful.

We shouldn't believe that we can't make any mistakes, but rather need to be willing to take the consequences and also take advantage of them when that happens.

As the saying goes, **making a mistake isn't a cause for worry; a cause for worry is when you start getting fond of the stone you're stumbling over.**

VI. No Country For Women.

Bad news isn't wine.
It doesn't improve with age.
COLIN POWELL

It was a perfectly cloudless, sunny day. The dry, golden fields were about to be harvested and the crickets were giving a concert. Although the heat was unbearable, it was good to be up on the Malpàs mountain, where I went to summer camp every year.

I was wearing short trousers that reached down over my knees, that showed my spindly legs, a long-sleeved yellow T-shirt that I was especially fond of, a cap with advertising on the peak, and my hair was cut very short.

I'd spent the afternoon hanging like a monkey, then crossing the top bar of the swings before heading for the swimming pool. One of the older monitors called me over. He spent quite a while telling me off, I can't remember whether it was because of the swings or something else. And when he'd finished, he said:

"Well now you know, Àngel. I hope I won't have to tell you again."

"Àngel?", I thought. "But I'm not Àngel, that's my brother!"

There was obviously very little difference between me and my brother.

Who's the leader?

Being the head of an expedition is, for some, and I would include myself among them, simply a formality written down on a piece of paper, an obligation which somebody has to take on. For others, it's like a medal they can stick on their chest and show off as if it were a status symbol, but in the end it really doesn't mean very much. It's just a name on a permit.

Let's not confuse the leader with the head of the expedition.

You will have the expedition head you've been assigned, because that's the person with the money who has set up the project, or because that's the person who's been given that particular job, but that doesn't mean that he or she is the leader by default.

As I mentioned in chapter II, **a leader is the person to whom you give your creativity, your efforts, your energy, your passion.** And you give all this voluntarily, because you believe in that person, because he or she has shown you how much commitment he or she has, and because you identify with that person's values and principles.

Expedition to K2

We were heading for K2, the second highest mountain in the world, along the Cassin Route, which is not the normal one. Once again, we were doing this with as little equipment and as few people as possible: no porters, no oxygen.

It had been my idea, so I was the one who had to deal with all the bureaucratic paperwork and who had to take on the role of expedition head. As I said before, I was simply the person whose name appeared on the documentation as a mere formality. When, years before, I'd gone to the north ridge along the so-called Japanese Route, on the Chinese side, the expedition head had been Héctor, and he did much the same then as I did now.

He was pleased as punch that he didn't have to do this arduous job again, and that it was my turn. But in Pakistan, which is where our current journey was taking us, I ran into an extra obstacle: that of being a woman.

Nine years earlier, I'd already been to this country, in the same Baltoro valley, also to climb a nearby mountain. And over the following nine years, things hadn't changed much for women.

Being a woman in Pakistan

In the rural villages, girls were banned from schools or found it extremely difficult to obtain access to them, and their lives were controlled by men from the moment they were born. Sometimes they were sold and given in marriage before puberty, and went to live with a husband who was often three times older than they were.

Their lives consisted of working at home and in the fields, and attending to and obeying their husbands. They had to get up before him and go to bed later than him. They often didn't eat at the same time, but rather did so after the men had eaten, making the best they could of the leftovers.

They couldn't show their faces in the street, where they had to walk behind the men. They were often victims of domestic abuse, of violence, and of rape, but it was almost impossible to report these crimes to the police, who usually refused to take down a statement; plus, there was a lack of medical personnel who could officially certify what had happened. On top of which, if, as happened in most cases, the victim didn't win the case – by law, she had to have four men as eyewitnesses – she would be accused of practising illicit sex or of adultery, a misdemeanour which was punished by stoning, although most times they went to jail...for having been raped!

On other occasions, when the victim was a little girl, she was forced to marry her rapist so as to erase the dishonour she had supposedly brought on her family. I'm describing a worst-case scenario. In the cities, things are a little different, but not enough to change this underlying reality.

The love of Captain Mustapha

Nine years earlier, I wasn't the head of the expedition, but I was the only one who spoke a little English; so I found myself acting as nothing more than an interpreter, in almost all the conversations between our expedition head and the military liaison officer, a twenty-four year old member of the army. Captain Mustapha came from Peshawar, the doorway to the Afghan border and a war zone.

I was twenty-one and during the two months that this journey lasted I became, without realising it, the Captain's intended bride. Any Pakistani officer liaising with an expedition, has, in theory, the job of facilitating its movements through military areas, acting as a go-between between you and the local residents, of giving you advice, of making sure that you climb the route for which you have a permit and, should he wish to, he even has the right to climb the mountain with you.

In reality, so Mustapha explained to us, all foreigners are potential spies. Which is why we are watched carefully in the Baltoro valley military zone, so that we don't go over to the Indians, with whom there is a permanent state of war involving confidential and strategic information.

There are also more than a few officers who will try and extort money from you, as was the case with some mountaineers whom we met, who had been threatened with an accusation of spying and immediate incarceration if they didn't pay the official in charge.

In that period, you could find yourself in jail before you'd even realised it.

Our officer turned out to be the most genuine, authentic soldier you could hope to meet. He was courteous, generous, polite and even amusing, but he had one single defect: he was determined that I marry him.

He asked me to on the return trip. At first I thought he was joking, but in the end I realised he was serious. I didn't know what to do, I said no and thanked him.

When we got to the first village and checked in to a hotel, he came into my room and insisted once more. He talked about Peshawar and the goats that he owned. Again, I thought that this was a joke, but when we reached Islamabad he gave me a metal wedding plate on which his name and mine were engraved, and that was when I started to panic. That man was absolutely certain that we would get married!

I was afraid that if I went on refusing, he would use the standard threat of that period and accuse me of 'being a spy'; that, added to me being a woman, would guarantee that I'd have a serious problem on my hands.

In the end, it all came to nothing. Maybe, more than anything else, it was just my mind playing games with me, who knows? Maybe the Captain regretted it all at the last moment, but at all events he let me leave the country without more ado.

All the same, I was on the receiving end of an amorous correspondence for the next two years. Letters to which I did not reply. My mother told me to think twice about it, that maybe I was missing an opportunity to make a fine match...

Return to Pakistan

And now I was back in Pakistan again, not uninfluenced by my memories and hoping that Mustapha had already found himself a wife. The new liaison officer, however, turned out to be another kettle of fish altogether.

Right from the start, he was overbearing, arrogant and unbending. I wonder of this attitude derived from the fact that he had to speak to and deal with me about anything to do with the expedition, something which probably, and even more in the case of a Pakistani officer, went against everything he'd been taught.

He tried to handle every consultation by talking to one of my male colleagues, instead of doing so with me, but without fail they would give him the cold shoulder and send him over to me.

At first, I felt quite uncomfortable. I had to work with someone who would not accept a woman as an equal, and even found it hard when I took decisions. It's difficult to carry out a project in which one of the participants, with whom you're working on a daily basis, hinders rather than helps.

The first part of the expedition was awful, and when everything got too much to bear, I ended up finding a way to face up to the problem and resolve the conflict.

In the first place, after days of what was nothing if not harassment, I had to get my self-esteem and self-confidence back. To learn not to underestimate myself, nor my skills, and how not to allow anyone to undermine my morale.

I'd never done so before, so why should I now let a Captain for the Pakistani army get away with it?

THE CHUTZPAH GAME

I often make out I've got a lot of chutzpah, sometimes quite openly and without any shame whatsoever. I even do this with things I know that I can't do and when it's obvious to everyone that I'm in over my head. A mathematical problem, a climb, a job, no worries...I can solve everything for you in a trice.

I've been doing this since I was little. At seven or eight I was forever competing with the boys in the class next door (at that time they still separated boys from girls). I competed with them to see who jumped the furthest or the highest or who was the fastest runner. I didn't have a clear perception or even the feeling that I wanted to compete and win, I just felt and still remember that there was no difference between us, and that there was no such thing as doubt. If they said they could do something, so could I.

By behaving in this way I taught myself not to have too many doubts about what I could do and what I couldn't. I taught myself to push myself beyond my own limits and to achieve better results than the ones I expected to have. And a consequence of that was that I believed and believe in myself more.

Us women often take for granted that we won't be able to do something, without even having tried to do it. Often that's a cultural inheritance, a tradition, given that even when we were very little we've been told that we can't do such and such a thing.

In the second place, I had to resolve the situation. If I'd left it to its own devices or waited for more time to pass, the situation wouldn't have improved or solved itself on its own. Quite the contrary, given time, my unease would have increased and I'd have lost any sense of objectivity.

Then came the moment I most feared: I had to have a complicated conversation with him.

When we have a problem we tend to go on the attack, but to resolve a conflict we need to talk. The night before doing so, I barely slept.

HOW TO ARGUE IN A POSITIVE WAY

There are difficult or uncomfortable conversations that need to be got through, because they're necessary. In order to get the best results...

-We need to limit the dialogue to one subject only and we have to have a clear idea of what that subject is. And we have to express what we want to say about it without the interference of any feelings or emotions.

-Most likely, we will have run through the conversation that we're going to have a hundred times in our head, and we think we know how the other person's going to reply. If you imagine that the conversation's going to be aggressive, instinctively the conversation you're going to have will tend to be that way. So try not to influence your thoughts, and if you have to do so, make sure it's in a positive way.

-Once we've said what we wanted to, we have to let the other party respond, without interrupting or coming up with new justifications and different arguments which will just confuse and sidestep the main issue. It's a mistake to jump at someone, without giving that person a chance to express him or herself.

-A confrontation doesn't have to become a fight. The other side can agree or disagree, but avoid entering into peripheral arguments which are beside the point. Negotiate, but don't fight. It's not a matter of trying to find out who's guilty or who is in the right, but rather of resolving and solving the issue which we're concerned with.

We will probably never become experts in dealing with confrontations, and nobody enjoys having them, but it's important not to steer clear of them when we have a hunch that something isn't right and doesn't fit in with the way things are supposed to be going.

Jeff, Jeff & Jennifer

I knew that I couldn't change the attitude of that man towards women, what with his own idiosyncrasies and his centuries-old cultural baggage. In fact, I had no intention of doing so. All I wanted to do was to get our project under way in the most harmonious manner possible.

It looked as if things had taken a turn for the better after our conversation, and we were able to go on climbing without that restless liaison officer saying no to everything and putting on a grumpy face every time he had to talk to me.

Our little expedition, made up of Héctor, Armando and myself, joined up with a small team from *National Geographic* magazine, consisting of Jeff, another Jeff and Jennifer. Only one of the Jeffs was a rock climber. Oddly enough, they were interested precisely in what people in this country found so hard to accept: the role of women, and in this case, that of a woman who was climbing a mountain and leading the project.

ENJOY PEOPLE AS THEY ARE

I have never stressed differences or felt different for being a woman, in either a negative or positive way. Simply because I don't believe in that, because that isn't in my mind-set or my behaviour. Because I've seen that a mountain is indifferent as to whether it is climbed by a man or a woman, and because I believe that if I decide not to think that something is the case, then often it isn't. That doesn't mean that I haven't had to make an effort on more than one occasion to demonstrate my skills and abilities, but I have these for professional reasons, not because I'm a woman.

You have to show a mountain that you can climb it. Do it properly, and it will let you. An initial effort doesn't mean that you have to be constantly obsessed about competing with the other sex and neither does it imply a rejection of help when it's offered to you. Too much mistrust or touchiness can lead to you cutting yourself off from the others. **You need confidence in what you are, clarity as regards what you want to achieve and the certainty that you will do your work well,** be you a woman or a man. Over the years, I've learnt to enjoy who I am.

The only K2 traitor

Towards the end of the expedition, Héctor, Jeff and I found ourselves facing that 8,611 metre high colossus; a battle of unequal forces awaited us.

We managed to bring all the material to Camp II, at 7,100 meters, in the middle of a storm, and then we returned to Base Camp.

When we had everything ready to make the final assault on the summit, the temperatures began to rise, against all the odds. One hot day followed another, and what we thought was good news turned out to be highly unfavourable to us.

As we climbed, it became an effort to unearth the ropes we'd installed, from under the ice, and some of them had been cut thanks to the stones that had fallen on top of them. The shining slope, completely bare of snow in which we could have marked out gradual steps that would have been comfortable to climb up, now required a tiring effort to climb.

As the hours passed, the heat melted more and more snow as well as the ice which held the rocks to the mountainside, which began to fall in our direction as if someone was playing Space Invaders with us. The first whizz of a falling rock caught us by surprise; the rocks that followed simply frightened us. We hid ourselves behind the few rocks that could protect us, and moved forward like patrol members in a war game

Until we brandished a white flag and began to retreat. That year we didn't reach the summit either. In fact, nobody would: not that year nor the next one.

Bodies under the ice

We didn't leave empty-handed. We hadn't reached the summit, but we did make a fairly interesting discovery.

One day, as Jeff and Jennifer were out walking, they found some human remains. The high temperatures had melted the ice and snow more than usual, exposing them to view.

While I wish to avoid being overdramatic, something I loathe, I must say that that year was especially rough as regards this particular matter. The bodies of several mountaineers who had disappeared over the previous years, came to light, including that of Renato Casarotto, the designer of the Magic Line, one of the most beautiful and difficult routes over this mountain. The bodies of three of the great Aragonese mountaineers - Javier Escartín, Javier Olivar and Lorenzo Ortiz - who died in 1995, along with the body of the New Zealander Bruce Grant, also appeared. As did those of the American called Rob, and of Alison Hargreaves, in my opinion the greatest Himalayan mountaineer ever, who were literally ripped off the ridge as they were descending it, by a strange burst of wind that came out of the blue.

After a couple of days of careful combing in order to confirm our suspicions, Jennifer ended up proving her theory: she'd found the remains of Wolfe. Dudley Wolfe was a wealthy American who had died while trying to climb this mountain in 1939.

Among the first set of remains there were some leg and hip bones, a piece of tent canvas and some tent poles, a cooking pot with a lid that said *Made in India*, something which confirmed the expedition had taken place before the partition of India and Pakistan in 1947. A little later, the remains of some trousers would be found, with a Cambridge badge on them, as well as a piece of legging and also some irrefutable evidence, which looked as if it had been left there by Dudley himself so that she could find it: a mitten bearing his name in capital letters. "WOLFE".

The puzzling story of Weissner and Wolfe

An astounding story took place here not long before the start of the Second World War, the Romantic era of the explorers, which involved a big controversy.

In 1939, an American expedition led by Fritz Weissner - a rock climber with exceptional skill for the time, a man who had climbed the most difficult rock faces then known - took up the challenge of climbing K2.

Until then, no mountain 8,000 meters high had yet been conquered. Wolfe formed part of this expedition as a member and also as a patron or sponsor. After a few months in the Himalayas and having spent two weeks without having climbed down from the mountain, Weissner, for the assault on the summit, solved the last of the difficulties to be faced on that mountain: the Bottleneck Couloir, by climbing it via a circuitous route along the rock.

All he had left to climb before reaching the summit was a snowy slope of just over 200 meters. He was at 8,385 meters when the Sherpa accompanying him, Pasang Lama, refused to continue, afraid they would have to spend the night in the open. Weissner had no choice but to turn back and give up his dream, so near and yet so far.

Lower down, in Camp VIII, at 7,800 meters, Wolfe had spent five days waiting for them. He'd managed to make it up there, even though the other members of his expedition - who regarded him as unskilled, and unprepared in terms of both experience and physical capability - thought he wouldn't be able to.

Wolfe waited for the return of his two colleagues until he was exhausted. His food supply had run out and he didn't have any matches left. To Weissner's surprise, Wolfe was quite alone. None of the Sherpas providing support were there, with whom Weissner had planned to make another assault on the summit, so all three decided to go back down to camp VII, further down.

When they got there, the camp was damaged, had no sleeping bags and was bereft of Sherpas. They spent the night as best they could and the next day Weissner and Pasang, seeing that Wolfe was in really bad shape, left him there and continued the descent as fast as they could to find the Sherpas so that the latter could get him down.

What they saw at the next camp was just as desolate. They spent the night there and then managed to get down to Base Camp.

Weissner was furious and couldn't understand why the camps had been dismantled. He sent three Sherpas up there and they found Wolfe at Camp VII, in an even more pitiable state, after having spent eight days there. He asked them to come back the following day, that by then he'd be ready to leave.

In that period, Sherpas were highly disciplined as far as orders from the patron were concerned, so without contradicting him, they went down to Camp VI. From that moment on, the rest of the story has been lost, given that nothing more was ever heard of them. The only thing known for certain was that K2 had claimed its first victims.

Weissner was severely criticised when he went back to the United States for having left Wolfe in Camp VII. For sixty-three years he was unable to satisfy his doubts about whether the Sherpas had tried to bring Wolfe down on the following day or if he had died during the descent or alone in the tent.

In 1993 the body of one of the Sherpas was found, that of Pasang Kikuli, while the other two remain inside the glacier. This find provided a little more information, maybe enough to conclude that Wolfe was in his tent when he died. So it's possible that the Sherpas had suffered an accident and had never managed to rescue him.

We told the family about this discovery, and finally it was decided to leave the remains at the Gilkey Memorial, at the base of K2, wrapped in Buddhist prayer blankets.

One last argument

When we finally got back to Islamabad, we had to have one last meeting at the Ministry and with the liaison officer so as to finish off the paperwork and go back home. And yes, here I have to confess that I lost my self-control, went apeshit or whatever you want to call it...And I ended up by making the liaison officer cry. I know that it's not a good thing for a 164 cm tall girl to make a Captain of the Pakistani army cry... I'm really sorry, I won't do it again.

VII. Amadablam and Meditation

We are shaped by our thoughts, we become what we think. When the mind is pure, joy follows like a shadow that never leaves.

BUDDHA

There were a few square meters of canvas on the ground, all of it clean and tidy. Outside all was quiet and none of my colleagues were inside; finally, no more smelly feet.

The two zips on the open doors let the last rays of sunlight into the tent, as well as the cold of the snow and the thin air. And all of this small space was mine and mine alone.

Alone in Camp II, at the top of a 5,900 metre tower, which is said to be one of the most beautiful mountains on the planet: the Ama Dablam, with a height of 6,856 meters.

This morning I left Base Camp accompanied by Miquel, but had to change plans when he didn't feel very well; I decided to continue on my own. It felt strange not having anyone with whom to comment on the scenery, the state of the route, or to plan what we would set out to do tomorrow. But I enjoyed and was grateful for this solitude, which was not at all lonely. As Moustaki says: **"No, I'm never alone, with my solitude."**

The next day I would go on climbing, all alone. At night I'd pass by Camp III, while a couple of expeditions there were still sleeping, and I'd make the ascent up to the summit via the final slope in the dawn light, trying to stay ahead of it with every tread I took, though I know the light always wins.

The meditation mountain

Mountain first appeared at a moment in my life when I was especially lost and confused: adolescence. I was attracted to them without really knowing why, I clung to them instinctively and stayed on them out of conviction. It's taken me a while to understand it all, but now I know why.

When I walk, when I climb, I take the most important steps in silence. The whole world disappears, the noises in my head go silent and the thousands of ideas that jump from one thought to the next, from the past to the future but skipping the present, quieten down.

Sometimes, my concentration is so great that I reach a point where I no longer exist, not me nor my concentration. Everything is will, conviction and awareness. At other times I only hear my own breathing, and I focus on the air that is entering and leaving my lungs. On occasion, I even have an incredible and indescribable sensation of love.

On Ama Dablam I discovered that the mountain has been and is a form of meditation and that many of the benefits I receive from it, are those brought about precisely by practicing meditation.

On that day, after climbing for six hours I reached Camp II, tidied it up and got everything ready to start climbing the following day. Then I sat at the door, with the zips open wide, and my feet hanging over the void. I look at the scenery, bare reality, without doing a thing, just breathing slowly and feeling how the pollution-free air of the Himalayas was reaching each and every one of the cells in my body.

This had happened to me at other times, but this time, maybe because I felt strengthened by the fact that I was alone and didn't have anyone to distract me, I started to concentrate and to take an intense interest in everything around me, with all its nuances. I lived through and enjoyed that moment, because it made the present stand out, that of my surroundings and that of my inner self.

TWO *MINDFULNESS* EXERCISES

The English term *Mindfulness* refers to the Vipassana, which was the main type of meditation taught by Buddha.

It translates as 'full attention' and we can define it as a way of becoming aware of the present, of what we are living and feeling from second to second, without judging it, without wanting to change it, accepting reality just as it is and observing it with all its subtleties.

This kind of meditation increases one's ability to face up to difficult situations, and not to react in an automatic fashion. We reduce anxiety, and gain concentration and tranquillity.

The goal of *Mindfulness* is to be fully aware for as long as possible, in the course of whatever we're doing during the day: writing, playing, shopping, waiting for the metro.

By being fully aware of what we're doing at any given moment, we accept it as it happens. **If our thoughts are elsewhere while we're doing something, we cease to enjoy the present, which is where happiness lies.**

The most popular technique when to comes to practising *Mindfulness* and one which coincides with other forms of mediation, is that of concentrating on breathing.

* Breathe in through your nostrils, exhale through your mouth. Concentrate on the sound and rhythm of the breathing. Let your abdomen expand instead of making your shoulders go up and down. At the beginning, and for the untrained mind, it can be difficult to hold one's attention for more than a minute. We need to rechannel our thoughts, which tend to run away and get distracted with other ideas, back to our breathing. Little by little and as we learn, our concentration will last longer.

* A second way of practicing *Mindfulness* is through conscious observation. Concentrate on any object around you: a pencil, a traffic light, a mountain, a bird, a park bench, a wastepaper bin. Don't study it, don't evaluate it, just observe it as it is. There needs to be a balance between observation and concentration.

When I left Camp I and started climbing, I had no idea which route I would follow up to the summit, because I'd never been to Camp III before. I would go up the mountain unaccompanied and in two stages instead of four.

All this was new for me, and more demanding in some respects than at other times. So with each step I took I made sure that I moved in a precise, fluid and well-judged way. My mind was focussed exclusively on this precise action and I went on like this for the five hours it took me to climb from Camp II to Camp III and then on to the summit, pausing briefly only to drink and radio back.

Time flew, and those five hours seemed very short. It was an effort that left my body tired and my mind as good as new.

What do I think about when I climb a mountain?

Sometimes I get asked that question, and on occasion I've asked myself the same question: "What do I think about for so many hours?"

I'm aware that I often don't think about anything at all.

While you're concentrating on your breathing, with each movement, each step, each action taken in the present moment, your thoughts stop jumping from one thing to another, they stop jabbering, they stop losing themselves.

Indeed, **it has been calculated that 45% of the time, our minds are distracted and lost in thought, and that that is a direct cause of unhappiness.** When looked at that way, you could say that for half our lives we are potentially unhappy.

By contrast, a calm, ordered mind is not only more efficient when it comes to taking decisions, it also activates the left side of the prefrontal cortex, which is responsible for positive emotions.

I was very close to the summit and extremely tired given that I'd merged two stages into one. I then had recourse to the strategy I've instinctively always used, so as not to think about who how tired I was or about the pain I felt.

When I couldn't concentrate on anything else, I counted my steps backward, from ten to one.

ATTENTION IS WHAT COUNTS

Counting is another exercise in concentration. It isn't one of the most elegant meditation exercises, but it's practical and is often used to teach the mind to stop thinking and thus getting distracted. For an athlete it would be the equivalent of weightlifting in order to improve his technique at any given sport: long jump, basketball, golf, etc.

As happens with breathing, we soon notice that our heads start thinking about something else. **The point of the training is to get the mind back to counting.** That instant when we realise we're starting to think about something else is when we strengthen the muscles of our concentration. If we fail to realise it, after two or three numbers, if we don't get back on track, we will probably end up thinking about something else.

Return to Base Camp

When I got to the summit I felt as if my mind were empty.

At some meditation retreats, three whole days are dedicated to emptying the mind, calming it completely and silencing it. Those meditating are not allowed to speak, read, use the phone or to have any other kind of intellectual stimulation.

That is quite similar to what happened to me in the course of my ascent of the mountain, given that as I'd been climbing over the last few days, I hadn't spoken, read, or had any other kind of intellectual stimulus. I'd spent many hours concentrating on each movement I made or on the scenery around me.

Compared to people who meditate, the only rule I hadn't obeyed was that of using the phone. If I hadn't radioed back to Base Camp, they'd have ended up having a heart attack.

On the way down, just before reaching the camp, I stopped for a moment and sat down on a large rock from which I could see the mountain and Base Camp at the same time. The simplest way to describe what I felt was an immense love, a huge affection for everything around me, for the people, my friends, the mountain, the country and even myself.

I climbed Ama Dablam to empty my mind, to fill up my heart.

THE PRACTICE OF EMPATHY

One *Mindfulness* exercise which is closely connected to Buddhism consists of training your compassion and sympathy at other people or the object on which you are focussing. ***Mindfulness* implies empathy.**

This involves self-implication, that is to say, observing ourselves as if we were somebody else and converting ourselves into an object of love or compassion, thus connecting us with our inner selves.

We wouldn't be doing the right kind of exercise if we concentrated on an object which made us angry or annoyed.

There are many activities which can produce this same state of concentration, as long as we are able **not to distract the mind with anything other than with what we are doing at that precise moment,** as these activities are also forms of meditation. A few examples: placing miniature ships inside a bottle; running; peeling potatoes; bowling; doing crochet; playing the piano; mowing the lawn; painting...You only have to search out these moments consciously to enjoy their benefits, because they and many other regular activities can help you meditate, alongside more traditional forms of meditation

The American psychologist Mihaly Csikszentmihaly calls this state of being *flow,* when a person flows during an activity, losing any sense of time and strengthening his or her skills and abilities as much as possible.

There are different schools of meditation, the main ones being Buddhist, Hindu and Taoist. Even so, meditation does not have to be linked with a religion. There are many kinds of meditation, aside from the Vipassana or *Mindfulness*. There are forms of meditation based on the repetition of a sound or mantra. Others are based on visualisation and others on the repetition of a movement. All forms of meditation have positive effects and different benefits.

La meditació, Various scientific investigations and medical tests have proven that meditation activates the left pre-frontal cortex, which is associated with positive emotions. It also activates the parasympathetic nervous system, which helps to improve the immune system. It increases serotonin, a neurotransmitter which is all but lacking in states of depression.

For all these reasons, meditation helps to fight stress, and to improve our concentration and our understanding of our goals. It provides emotional intelligence, motivation, balance, and makes us more productive and creative. In business, it helps us concentrate when dealing with a complicated deal, and makes students more efficient.

To meditate is to cultivate the mind and the heart.

I approached the mountain without really knowing why I was doing so. I went ahead instinctively and stayed there out of conviction. It's taken me a while to understand it all, but now I know why.

I went to the mountain, and now I'm trying to bring the mountain back home.

VIII. Training the Body and the Mind

Every day, the most difficult battle I fight is the one against myself.

NAPOLEON BONAPARTE

The wounds on my ankles which I'd caused, yet again, were bleeding again. This time more blood was flowing than when the wound was fresh.

Time after time the screw which served to adjust my old strap-on skates got loose or got lost, and with my tiny fingers I spent hours trying to fit it into place, in vain. So the straps were often loose and that's why I kept hurting my ankles. To make sure the skates didn't slip off me, I tightened the straps – to which I'd added extra holes - so much that they put my feet to sleep.

When I went to play in the street, or while I was running along the corridor at home, I would yell:

"Mum, I'm off to my training!"

And I'd slam the door shut. With the skates in my hands, I went down the four flights of stairs, taking them two by two, because I wasn't allowed to use the lift on my own. But I was allowed to skate down the street kamikaze style without anyone saying a word. I would disappear every afternoon to start the scrupulously planned training schedule that I'd been devising all morning.

That summer of 1976, the Montreal Olympics were on the telly, and I was six. I remember seeing Nadia Comaneci win a gold medal for her routine on the uneven bars; she was awarded a perfect ten.

I became fascinated by sports gymnastics and wanted to show my mother that I could do them too. I called her to the living room, did a Handstand and fell flat on my back onto the floor. She didn't say much, she raised her eyebrows, muttered "Yes, yes, yes..." and went back into the kitchen, still drying the plate she was holding.

I spent five minutes stretched out unable to breathe and that was that. At home, they couldn't afford to send me to a private sports centre to learn gymnastics or skating.

The city as a training field

My hands were burning and my fingers were opening up. The pain was so great that I couldn't take it anymore, but had to hold out for a little longer. I had to let pass another thirty seconds until I could let go of the bar from which I'd been hanging for quite a while.

The gymnasium was small, a little room on the municipal sports grounds in the Parc del Migdia where I'd been training almost every morning for the last two years before heading for the university. When I left home I would walk for a while and then take the metro, ten stops and one change. When I came out, I would run the 500 meters to the Avinguda de la Reina Maria Cristina. Then I'd go up the

322 steps that led to the Olympic Stadium, I'd never use the escalators, it was against my religion.

Often, when I pass by there, I think about the 1992 Olympic Games. I watched them from Nepal, not long before we started to climb the Shishapangma; I was in a tiny, humble village in which the family that lived there had electricity, a satellite dish and a TV which was used by the entire village.

As I watched, I thought about how my own sport would never win an Olympic medal. That gave me a feeling of relief, maybe like that of a multimillionaire when he says to his girlfriend, after some time, that he's rich and knows that she loves him for who he is and not for his money.

Finally, from there I would do the last 800 meters before reaching the park. One hour there and one hour back, three times a week. Only once did I succumb to the temptation of returning by car, but it was worth it: the person giving me a lift was the Formula One driver, Pedro Martínez de la Rosa. Sometimes we trained at the same time, and when we got home I'd look at him and say:

"Your car isn't exactly anything special."

And I'd thank him, with an ironical smile.

Sometimes all this coming and going across Barcelona, the routine of the gymnasium, the pain, getting up early and not being able to get up late at weekends made me feel like giving the whole thing up. This feeling would last a few split seconds, and only came very rarely.

It would have been a problem if this kind of thought had been more persistent, but I used a couple of tactics to make sure that wouldn't happen: certain tools to motivate myself.

SELF-MOTIVATION

The main key is to **break your routine.** Never to do the same training, with the same people. **Introduce variations, creativity and fun.** Use different places and different techniques.

In my case, I varied my activities, by running, rock climbing, skiing, swimming, going to the gym, etc.... which had an advantage aside from the obvious one of breaking the monotony and not being tedious, which was that like this we learn more and acquire more skills, which can be applied when things turn out differently from what we're used to.

A day-to-day example: by obliging yourself to meet up with another person, it will be impossible for you to disappoint the other person and by extension to disappoint yourself.

Another useful tool for increasing self-motivation is that of **competitiveness.** Healthy competition among colleagues, as in a game, is stimulating and helps us to slowly improve ourselves, to be better. I don't need to say that if this kind of competition leads to quarrels and is no fun at all, then it doesn't make any sense. Our competitors must be our rivals, not our enemies.

We have to be realistic when it comes to **setting our goals, which shouldn't be too easy or too difficult, but just a little beyond our current capabilities.** When it comes down to it, this requires some humility, because it's possible that we aren't as good as we would like to be, and being realistic means accepting that fact. If you set a goal that is beyond your capabilities, you will probably have to give up half way through. On the other hand, **we mustn't set targets that are less demanding than what we're ready and willing to do**, because if we achieve something that doesn't require an effort, we won't enjoy doing it and it won't mean much to us. Which is why it's important to **know oneself, be realistic, and set a goal that we find demanding**, that obliges us to make an effort which will make us feel satisfied and which we won't give up on.

Setting short-term goals will help us get results within the framework of an overall objective. There is nothing more demotivating than not seeing concrete results or not being informed as to whether what we are doing works or is leading nowhere.

But self-motivation can go much further. Mastering techniques and knowing how to put them into practice can be very useful in that we will end up liking something which, at first, we hadn't so much as dreamed of doing. This often happens, and not just in training sessions, but also in life and at work. **Our choice of attitude can help us to enjoy what we're doing.**

In their book *Fish!* STEPHEN C. LUNDIN, Harry Paul and John Christensen explain how a fisherman can introduce creativity, games and fun into his work routine, and can end up spreading this positive attitude to others, thus ensuring success. In the words of the authors themselves: "**Find ways to *play*. We can be serious about our work without being serious about ourselves. Stay focussed in order to *be*** *present* when your customers and team members most need you. And should you feel your energy lapsing, try this sure-fire remedy: find someone who needs a helping hand, a word of support, or a good ear – and *make their day."*

I forget I have habits

I prepared my bag just as I did every Wednesday. A drink, my metro card, a book, a clean T-shirt and a small towel. I left home and headed down the street.

Once I was in the metro I noticed that there was something odd. It was almost empty, given that it was a work day. When I got the end of my journey and went out onto the street, I had the same impression. It was like the world had come to an end.

When I arrived at the gymnasium, I realised what had happened: it was a public holiday and so there was no training session. Well, as I'd come all this way, at least I could run a couple of laps on the athletics track.

Going out to run, brushing our teeth, going to a training session, all become habits, a routine which we go through automatically, without any or very little effort. Throughout the day, there are routines which we complete, some of them healthy and others which aren't, really, and which we would like to get rid of.

The importance of the thought activator

Let's first take a look at how we create a habit. For example, let's suppose we want to go out and exercise every day, or have a daily studying routine, or any other of the New Year resolutions we say we're going to stick to.

The two main tools required to create a habit are **motivation** and what is known as a **thought activator.** Some authors add that a given skill is also necessary, but I don't agree. I don't think it's indispensable.

It would be logical to think that if we often don't consolidate a habit it's because we don't have enough motivation, and that that is where we have to expend all our energy. But that isn't really the case. **Where we have to expend our energy in order to create a habit has to do with the thought activator.** This activator is nothing more than a way of reminding ourselves and obliging ourselves to do that which we wish to become a habit which we can't avoid doing. We invent it ourselves.

If we want to go running every morning, we can put some sports shoes at the foot of the bed, in a place where we can't help but see them when we get up. Or we can oblige ourselves to meet up with someone.

If we want to study when we get back from school, we can hide away the TV's remote control or the TV itself, or meet up with people so as to work together. It's a matter of creating the activator that we want to have, and the more persuasive it is, the less we will fail until the habit is fully consolidated.

Abandoning negative habits

Breaking or getting rid of unwanted habits is more complicated. When we eliminate an unwanted habit, it leaves a vacuum. If we don't fill it with some other habit, the one we have got rid of will install itself again, re-occupying that vacuum. So the most practical thing is to substitute it with something healthier, to put something in place instead of the bad habit.

If we want to stop eating chocolate when we sit down to watch TV, we can prepare some slices of carrot or apple. If we want to stop going into Facebook all the time, we can put a notebook next to the computer on which we can write or draw.

To sum up: **for every habit we wish to eliminate, we need to find a heathy substitute.**

Normally, we need a month for a habit to become automatic. But there is no exact time limit, as it depends on the difficulty of the new habit, on the time we spend on it, and on how it interferes or adapts itself to our daily life.

SEVEN KEY FACTORS WHEN IT COMES TO CREATING A POSITIVE HABIT

—Let's not forget the magic ingredient: the activator.

—We should repeat the action <u>every day.</u> If we only do it two or three times a week, it'll be difficult to make it work.

—Being coherent helps the habit: it should always be done at the same time, always in the same way, always in the same place. Variations do not help.

—Start with a little and go on to do more.

—Eliminate any nearby temptations.

—Having a model to follow nearby can help us achieve our goal.

—If you start thinking you won't be able to do it, think of it as an experiment. Experiments never fail, they simply give different results.

The other muscle that needs training: willpower

We can define will power as the ability to resist minor temptations and overcome obstacles in order to achieve an objective in the long term: our goal. **Willpower can control our thoughts, our feelings and our actions.**

Often, when we don't achieve what we've set out to do, we conclude that it's because we don't have enough willpower. We tend to think that it's an inexhaustible source of energy, and that whoever has it never fails. But **willpower is like any other source of energy, it drains away little by little in the course of the day.** Stress, taking decisions, saying no again and again to a temptation will result in a lack of willpower if we overdo things.

Recent studies have shown that willpower is like a muscle that can be trained to make it stronger and capable of lasting over many kilometers, given that if it is weak and you ask too much of it, it will become impaired.

Research carried out by Roy Baumeister at the University of Florida with two groups of young people turned out to be very interesting in this regard. The students who practised self-discipline and willpower got better results with their studying, went to class more often, and consumed less alcohol and drugs. A self-discipline test involving these students turned out to be a better predictor of academic success than an IQ test.

There were two control groups, one involved with sports and the other with finance. The first followed a training programme for resistance and energy. When it was over, the students got better results in the self-discipline test, got better results in class, smoked less, drank less alcohol and ate less junk food. And perhaps you'll say: that's because they're practising sports. Certainly it can look that way, but it turned out that they also watched less TV, did more homework and tidied up their rooms more.

As for the finance-related group, the students had to manage their finances over four months using a particular system. The result was that they not only increased their savings considerably, but their studying improved, as did their contributions to household chores; and they also consumed less tobacco.

Self-control and willpower exercises are not specific to any given field. This is muscle training that can be applied later to many different tasks.

What's more, research has demonstrated that people with greater willpower don't spend their time fighting off temptations. Instead of that, they create a lifestyle for themselves in which they are less exposed to such distractions and to the exhaustion that they cause.

Visualising

I got up suddenly, my heart thumping, and called out, frightened because a dog had bit my neck. I put my hand on my neck. There was nothing there, just the feeling of me pressing it while I clenched my teeth.

It was just a dream, I was asleep, but it was as if it were real. On other occasions I recall the Everest avalanche and wonder what would have happened if, instead of it moving in another direction, it had carried me off.

In less than a second my heartbeat accelerates, my mouth dries up and I get into a panic: nothing is happening, not at that moment, but by imagining it I make my mind and body believe that it really is happening right now.

How come I can feel all that, even though it hasn't happened, as if it were real? Because I visualise.

THE POWER OF VISUALISATION

Dr. Maxwell Maltz says something to the effect that **our brain doesn't distinguish between a real event and an imaginary one.** Which is why our bodies send signals and react almost in the same way to a thought (a subjective reality) as they do to things which really happen (objective realities). So our bodies send out orders for endorphins, neurotransmitters, hormones, etc. to be secreted, be they prejudicial or beneficial, almost in the same way as if something were really happening.

Aside from the physical response, imagining an event can also influence our psychological response and condition our behaviour and attitude.

How many times have we told ourselves that we can't do something? If you convince yourself that you can't do it, you won't be able to. But the opposite thought – that you can do it – if accompanied by a visualisation of how you can do it and the feeling of achieving what you want to, is a lot more beneficial.

This kind of thinking makes the difference between trying to do something and never doing it. It calls for an effort, but it can be done. Maybe at first things won't turn out too well for us, but later things will improve. Making a move, carrying out an action in our minds helps us to achieve what we want to. **It doesn't come for free, there's no magic involved, everything requires an effort, all you have to do is practice.**

A few days ago I did an in-depth repetition of this mental visualisation exercise in order to put together a for me extremely difficult competitive rock-climbing route ('Qui c'est cette lolotte', Camarasa, 7c+).

I closed my eyes and went through each stage of my actions. I placed myself in front of the route and knew that I would reach the top. I checked the rope and knot. I was carrying everything I needed: climbing harness, rock climbing shoes, helmet. I put magnesium on my hands, breathed in and set off, convinced I would reach the top without falling. Mentally, I remembered the full sequence of movements, each one of between 60 to 70 steps, and I did them all perfectly. I placed my feet correctly in each of the holds. I remembered exactly where to put each hand, and how my fingers moved when the hold was vertical, or small, or to one side. I felt myself take a firm hold. The sequence was fluid and there were no mistakes, no doubts, no fear and I took pleasure in each movement.

I repeated this visualisation several times, with all the movements and feelings involved, and the result was always the same. Everything was in my head: I imagined what I wanted to; I imagined and felt I would win.

After doing this for six nights in a row, I finally went and did the route I'd planned on doing, and as if by magic, everything turned out just as I had envisioned. I managed to go through all the moves in a clean, calm fashion. Even my colleague on the rope was surprised that things turned out so well for me, this being the first time I'd touched the wall after a week of not being near it.

The Australian psychologist Alan Richardson carried out a little experiment in this regard. She took three groups of basketball players. The first had to practise three-point shots for twenty minutes a day. The second group had to visualise the shots without training, and the third group didn't have to do anything, neither training nor visualising. The result was impressive: the second group got results that were almost as good as those of the first, whereas the results of the third group were dismal.

In order to visualise, we need to be in a quiet room or space. We need to close our eyes, take a couple of breaths and start to project our minds towards what we want to happen.

First, we should imagine the place: where we are and what we want to do. If we have to do an exam, give a lecture or play the piano, in the latter case we have to imagine the piano, the keys, the chair, the concert hall and the atmosphere in as much detail as possible.

Then we have to imagine ourselves doing the action itself: the way our hands touch, in just the way we want them to, smoothly, without mistakes, without fear, without nervousness. If we have to do an exercise, we should try and reproduce it as precisely as possible. **Feeling one's emotions in a positive way is very important.**

What we do when we visualise is to **strengthen and reinforce a skill in our minds,** outside the location where it would normally take place, without our brain realising that we aren't there. We control and decide the outcome of our actions. **Visualising doesn't do the work itself, but it improves it.**

After visualising my first 8a (5.13b in USA scale) rock climb, I've often visualised other things. The most recent has been how to finish the following chapter, number nine, "After Everest", the last one in the book. I visualise myself sitting at my office desk looking at the mountains and typing at the computer. The words flow, disordered thoughts slowly begin to take shape. I watch as I deliver the chapter to the publisher in time without getting stressed and feel satisfied with the work I've done.

IX. After Everest

Try not to become a man of success, but rather try to become a man of value.

ALBERT EINSTEIN

That guy was looking at my project with a sceptical face. I never knew if he understood what he was reading. I didn't stay long enough to find out. His last question allowed me to make an excuse and put an end as quickly as possible to that fruitless meeting, to which I would never go back...and I'm grateful to him for that.

"Sure, OK, that's fine, but aside from climbing this 8,000 metre high mountain alpine-style, without oxygen, or Sherpas, or ropes, or anything...Are you going to do it with a blind person...or something else that will make it a bit spectacular?

"Yes, of course, I'll climb it wearing red knickers if that's what you want." I thought, without saying a word as I looked at him with raised eyebrows and a thin smile.

The Everest trap

I spent several weeks turning things over in my mind, not because I was weighing up my choice of option, but because there was something amiss. I had that niggling feeling in my head, a soft-spoken voice that was telling me something wasn't right. I'd had it for some time: it was the unease which was changing the happy person I'd always been into someone who woke up and went to bed with a phantasmagorical sense of worry, an internal struggle that was starting to make me feel worn out and empty.

After mulling it over for a long time, and chatting with a couple of good friends, I ended up discovering that the answer to my uneasiness, deep down, was relatively simple: I wasn't doing what I really wanted to do. Once I'd climbed Everest, with all the consequent media fuss that I'd never expected and had never gone looking for, out of inertia I'd done what I'd supposed I had to keep on doing: climb 8,000 metre high mountains, making it into a spectacle, if possible. And that couldn't be further from the way I thought of this sport.

That doesn't mean that I was forced to take part in the expeditions to 8,000 metre mountains that I went on after Everest. I either planned them or invited myself along and I was convinced that that was what I wanted.

However, little by little and without realising it, I was focussing increasingly on my real passion: alpine style climbing. Although I'd faced the challenges of the Himalayas using this lightweight, compromising style, the sole, exclusive ascent to summits 8,000 meters high had never been my main priority, but rather had been something complementary.

The lonely alpine routes, even though they are possibly more technically difficult and spectacular than the normal routes of some 8,000 metre mountains, have no media impact whatsoever, and therefore receive no sponsorship whatsoever.

And here I found myself face to face with a contradiction which had possibly been the source of my internal conflict: that of wanting or not wanting a sponsor, of playing the media's publicity game and everything that went with it, or abandoning it.

I should add that much of this dilemma wouldn't have existed if I'd come from a wealthy family, because then I could have organised my expeditions where and how I wished and off I'd go. But, like most people, I had to factor economic survival into the equation of my plans.

A personal road map

On a piece of paper, a most useful and economic utensil, I made a list, in different columns, of the pros and contras of each different situation. Like that, I could evaluate what I would decide to do, in a way that was more visual and graphic.

The alternatives were as follows: if I wanted a more comfortable life, I would have to accept certain inconveniences, or to put it another way, in order not to have to cope with certain inconveniences, I would have to plan my projects in a more individual, almost home-made way. That would be satisfying, as I would have to weigh up all the odds and choose my own objectives.

Everybody looks for different things in their lives and daily activity so as to get some satisfaction from them, and all options are perfectly legitimate. The person who climbs the South Face of the Shishapangma along a one-off route in the alpine style isn't looking for the same experience as someone who climbs the North Face by the normal route in the classic style and with the backing of a sponsor. They're two different needs, two different productions, two different markets.

Separating my mountaineering completely from media attention and sponsorship didn't take a week or a month, but a little longer.

In the end it turned out that that meeting with the man who wanted me to climb the mountain with a blind person, wasn't completely useless. Certainly, you could say that I came out of that meeting empty-handed, but when I closed that door I realised the meeting had helped me realise what it was I really wanted and how I could be consistent with my thoughts.

Sometimes, for a thing like that to happen, something has to kick-start or hasten events.

Gauguin had been a stockbroker and an amateur painter who worked at the Paris Stock Exchange. After the 1882 crash, his boss fired him. When he did so, Paul Gauguin got up out of his chair and gave him a big, grateful hug, because he sensed that this would be the first day of what was left of his life.

	Possibility of success	Possibility of finding a sponsor	Media impact	Dependency on or links to media	Economic benefits	Satisfaction
Climbing 8000m summits via normal route and classic style with sponsor	high	good/high	high	high	good/high	low
Climbing 8000m summits via technical routes in alpine style with sponsor	low	good/low	good	high	little	good
Climbing 8000m summits via technical routes in alpine style without a sponsor	low	good/low	low	none	little/none	good
Climbing alpine routes around the world without a sponsor	low	low/none	low/none	none	none	excellent

FOUR KEYS TO THE RESOLUTION OF INTERNAL CONFLICTS

—**Realising that there's something inside us that's not going well** is a good first step. Just as in other circumstances that I've mentioned in earlier chapters, being aware is a good way to start fighting a situation that isn't any good. We often want to convince ourselves that it'll pass, that it's nothing, that it's all nonsense. But our niggling feeling doesn't go away. What's more, it ends up being a tougher struggle than one involving a normal problem, because in this fight we're struggling on our own.

—It's possible that the most important step is that of **telling someone about it**: a friend, a partner, a professional... It isn't unusual to run into people who have been blocked for years. To hold out for so many years without solving a conflict can bring about a severe internal fracture, and lead to a serious depression. Sometimes the more important or influential the person, the more he or she will hide the fact that there's a part of their life which hasn't been resolved and that they need help. We all need help at some time in our lives. Nobody's perfect, and nobody is going to reject us or despise us because we need that help.

—Internal conflicts can appear **when our actions don't correspond to our thoughts or values** and when we deny this in a conscious or subconscious way.

—He need to **find the reason for this.** We can look for it by writing or by talking to a colleague or to a professional. We write so as to give voice to our thoughts. The more we write, the more thoughts will emerge, and all of them will be good. We need to write down anything that comes to mind, without any shame, given that nobody's looking at us. Some of these thoughts will end up giving us an idea of what is really happening within ourselves.

A plan of action

After this decision to break with the original mountaineering project, little by little I began to work out a professional strategy.

I've never stopped mountaineering. I couldn't. Be it far away or close to home, with less or more money, sharing expenses or heading off on my own in a van, I need it. I go the mountains in the same way everybody does, the way I'd always done: with my own money, without expecting anything in return and without any ostensible motives.

Of the over thirty expeditions which I've done so far, seven have been sponsored and only one resulted in a direct economic payment: the salary I was paid to do the **IMAX** Everest documentary. Despite the many expeditions I've done, I do not consider myself a mountaineering professional. Football professionals are paid to both play and train; joiners are paid to both design and make furniture; lawyers, to prepare a defence and then put it into practice during a trial.

They don't pay me to either train or climb, quite the opposite.

I wanted to keep on having a professional connection with mountaineering, but, paradoxically, also to be directly disconnected from it. So, how could I work out a coherent plan of action? How could I take on this project without again feeling that something wasn't right? Well, by making use of my talent and following my passion.

Talent and passion

Over several years, I'd developed a certain talent for communication. I like explaining things and I knew how to structure such explanations in a reasonably understandable way.

A few months after the launch of the Everest documentary, an American company asked me to give a motivational talk to its employees. I read up on what kind of concepts could fit in to my lecture and also thought about my own experiences. Over the years, I ended up developing an interesting career as a lecturer.

In this way, I was still connected to mountaineering as a form of work, but indirectly. My speaking engagements reached out into different fields, such as television, the press, and radio, all of them linked to sports, mountaineering and health. I didn't accept some TV work, given that my safety alarm went off before I could fall into traps which I was already partly familiar with. Convictions versus actions.

I don't regard myself as being especially talented when it comes to artwork but that together with mountaineering make up my two great passions. In fact, I can't remember which came first, drawing or sport.

Following one's vocation

I would jump with the same energy that I spent when paddling a canoe, but instead of being nine I might have been four.

How come I can remember that? I don't really know, but maybe because in a neighbourhood sack race I won a box of six Jovi brand watercolours, of which I even remember the smell. I was the happiest little girl in the world, possessor of a priceless treasure. I ran home to put them to good use and since then I've never stopped painting or drawing.

Just as with mountaineering, I submerge myself into a world in which I disconnect from reality, in which every stroke, every line, every touch of the brush or mixture of colours provides me with moments of total concentration.

I made a big mistake when I was a teenager: not to follow-up this passion professionally. Without any points of reference of my own, without enough force to impose my will, I went along with and believed the advice of the family, which was based more on rumour than anything else and was very common at the time, that said: "You won't be able to make a living from that." That is why I put my first vocation to one side and substituted it for another one, which was also fine by me.

Nowadays, I talk to teenagers who are studying a subject at university or who are about to choose one, and I've found that not everybody has a passion. There's nothing that makes them especially passionate. So they choose to do something they're just pretty good at.

The two questions

I few years ago, in Peru, on the stage where I was giving some talks, I met an excellent communicator, Tal Ben-Shahar. He is a Harvard professor and the author of several books, such as *Happier: Learn the Secrets to Daily Joy and Lasting Fulfilment* or *The Pursuit of Perfect: How to Stop Chasing Perfection and Start Living a Richer, Happier Life,* who had managed to make his classes the most popular in the entire history of the university. His main theme is positive psychology, in which, in broad terms, he advises people **to look for what you do well rather than analyse what you do badly** because if you only ask yourself about what isn't working, you'll only see what isn't working.

Ben-Shahar asked his students two questions.

"What gives you strength and energy?"

"What are you good at?"

He says that we all have a talent, what he called "the seed". Many have yet to discover it, but once you do discover it it must be appreciated and used frequently.

He also says that **30 minutes of exercise three times a week has the same effect as the strongest medicine.** It reduces Parkinson's and dementia by 52% and makes us smarter (though I'm not sure that this last point is true in my case ☺).

Although I fully agree with Ben-Shahar, I don't believe that talent and passion always go together. Which is why I think the best gift life can give you is passion, but not necessarily talent.

Tina & Shirtas

The mountains of the world are my first love. This same passion led me to constantly wanting to be learning something: like how to paint with acrylic instead of watercolour, designing web pages, doing kiteboarding, creating apps for tablets and smartphones, etc.

If we always do the same things, without modifying our activity, whether to vary it or to adapt it to changing times, tools and formats, we run the risk of becoming obsolete. Mark Twain said that the **person who stops learning, grows old**, be he twenty or eighty years old, whereas those who continue to learn stay young. So the best thing you can do is to learn and keep your mind young.

Aside from working for others as a communicator, I wanted to start up my own company, in keeping with my concept of indirect mountaineering. There I would put together my wish to convey ideas with my passion for illustration, and so I created two projects:

Tina's Journey (**www.tina.cat**).

This is a series of children's stories (in Catalan and Spanish) in which the main character is a blue-haired girl who travels around the world climbing mountains and practising different outdoor sports.

With the excuse of looking for something on each journey, these voyages teach her values and principles, from sport to getting along with people from different countries. Tina discovers legends, religions, cultures, sometimes magical worlds...and at other times a little science.

Tina is an educational project with an infinity of possibilities that go beyond the current collections, called "About the Seven Summits" and "Parks and Outdoor Spaces". It is a window open to my creativity and the need to contribute something; Tina has offered me an opportunity to realise myself.

—*Shirtas* (**www.shirtas.com**).

This is my most mischievous escape valve. A virtual store for T-shirts carrying designs by me which can be themed or absurd, and which hide a message or a double meaning. Conceptually, the idea began in one of the hidden valleys of the Himalayas, the Shirtas valley.

Mountains of life

After all this, I have gone back to my first love, with a freedom which I once believed I'd lost.

In Patagonia, after having climbed the Exocet Chimney on Cerro Standhart, I saw the amazing illuminated spectacle when the first light of day lit up the peaks of Cerro Torre.

In Mali, after opening up a new route on the Hand of Fatima, my heart shrunk when I saw the poverty of that country embodied by a naked boy not much older than two, who was begging for food in the streets with a little empty cup in his hands.

In the Alps, I've trembled from the cold when abseiling in the night after having climbed the Aiguille Verte, the Bonatti, or the Gran Capuccin or the Piz Badile.

In Iran I was surprised by the energy of the women. Although they had to be all wrapped up, we dedicated a 650 metre rock climbing route which they inaugurated, to them and their difficult circumstances; the route was called Different Problems.

In Canada I've heard the wolves serenade us after we climbed up the ice of the Pomme d'Or.

On Montserrat, I've climbed with Eric, the first blind person to climb Everest, and I learnt that I don't see too well myself.

In Lebanon we crossed the mountain range from north to south on skis, without a map, and taking care not to tread on any mines. We chatted and drank with the border soldiers and ended up sleeping in a brothel.

In the Pyrenees I've been happy, because you can feel just as small close to home as you can in the Himalayas.

And yet other mountains have come along, more repetitions of routes and more openings of others which maybe nobody else will ever take. Maybe nobody will ever know we've been there, nor what we did there, not who we are, but, as Ralph Waldo Emerson said: "Success consists in obtaining what you wish for; happiness, in enjoying what is obtained."

After everything

When I got back from Everest, I was quite literally aphonic after two weeks of doing an average of four or five daily interviews. In each one, I took special care to make it very clear that my 1996 Everest ascent, done in the classic style, along the usual route and forty-six years after it had been climbed for the first time, made me very happy, but didn't bring anything new to mountaineering.

Not one media outlet broadcast these thoughts of mine. On the contrary, the most romantic ones crowned me "the queen of the Himalayas, of the mountain"; the more inaccurate ones as the "queen of mothers"; and the most sensationalist ones described me as the heroine of a fierce struggle with the world's highest peak.

This... I don't know what to call it, maybe a tendency to make everything seem more dramatic than it really is, to create heroes, myths, this need to exaggerate, this insistence on making out that things are more difficult, greater, tougher and more complicated than they really are, doesn't help at all.

I prefer to see both our goals and life itself as a summit which we can reach, by climbing in small steps, making an effort, with a sense of humour, enjoying the moment, sharing and learning; a summit which doesn't need to be that high, nor that difficult to reach.

The steps to the summit

I can't do this

I like it, what should I do?

I want to do it, I will try

I think I can get it

Yes, I know I will get it

I got it

let's go for the next

BIOGRAPHY

Araceli Segarra was born in Lleida, Catalonia Alpinist. Children's book Illustrator . Speaker. Writer. Occasional model. TV host. Graduated in Physiotherapy.

Ms. Segarra began in mountain sports at age15 with a spelunking course, she continued exploring the outdoors through Randonnée skiing, rock climbing and ice climbing.

In 1996 she became the first Spanish woman to climb Mont Everest. Her ascent was chronicled in the IMAX documentary EVEREST. On the same expedition, she was a member of the rescue team during the worst disaster in the history of Mount Everest, when 13 people died, credited with the idea of marking a rescue helicopter landing location with an "X" made of red Kool-Aid.

She has since worked in media (national geographic, discovery channel or 7 years in Tibet) and communications, publishing a series of illustrated children's books: Tina's Journey. **www.tina.cat** And delivered more than 200 motivational conferences around the world for international companies.
In addition, she has participated in more than 30 climbing expeditions, some of them to open new routes.

Her first book "Not that high and Not that difficult" addressed to the business environment, sport and personal growing, has been published in Spanish, Catalan and Italian. More than 25.000 books sold.

Also, the complete series of "Tina at the 7 summits" has been translated to Chines.

She explores her art passion with her SHIRTAS brand, where she designs mountain clay jewellery & T-shirts

www.tina.cat

Index

Made in the USA
Middletown, DE
10 May 2021